Designing Learning for Tablet Classrooms

Donovan R. Walling

Designing Learning for Tablet Classrooms

Innovations in Instruction

Springer

Donovan R. Walling
Bloomington, IN, USA

ISBN 978-3-319-02419-6   ISBN 978-3-319-02420-2 (eBook)
DOI 10.1007/978-3-319-02420-2
Springer Cham Heidelberg New York Dordrecht London

Library of Congress Control Number: 2013957429

Printed on acid-free paper

Springer is part of Springer Science+Business Media (www.springer.com)

Acknowledgments

In developing this book, I have been fortunate to be able to tap the expertise of a number of colleagues, prominent among them Phillip Harris, executive director of the Association for Educational Communications and Technology; retired Bloomington, Indiana, educator Joan Harris; Mark Gage, director of publishing and digital content at the Center for Civic Education; Henry Borenson of Borenson and Associates, Inc.; Kenneth Rosenberg, a graduate student at Indiana University; Jonas Beier, a graduate student at the Johannes Gutenberg University of Mainz, Germany; Florida elementary special needs educator Connie Huston; Bloomington, Indiana-based learning designer Michael Shermis; and Niklas Everling, a high school student in Bremen, Germany. I also am grateful for the support and encouragement of my partner, Sam Troxal.

Contents

About the Author

Donovan R. Walling is a writer and editorial consultant. He also is a senior consultant for the Center for Civic Education and formerly was director of publications for Phi Delta Kappa International. Prior to moving into education publishing, he was a curriculum administrator in public school districts in Wisconsin and Indiana, following a lengthy career as a classroom teacher in Wisconsin and for the US Department of Defense in Germany.

Walling is the author or editor of 16 books. Recent titles include *Why Civic Education Matters; Writing for Understanding: Strategies to Increase Content Learning; Teaching Writing to Visual, Auditory, and Kinesthetic Learners; Visual Knowing: Connecting Art and Ideas Across the Curriculum; Public Education, Democracy, and the Common Good;* and *Virtual Schooling: Issues in the Development of E-Learning Policy.* He also has contributed articles to a number of professional journals, including a six-part series on student-produced media, titled "Tech-Savvy Teaching," for the Association for Educational Communications and Technology (AECT) journal, *TechTrends.* He is the coauthor (with Phillip Harris) of "Policies Governing Educational Technology Practice and Research" (Chap. 50) in *Handbook of Research on Educational Communications and Technology, Fourth Edition.* He also edits and designs the AECT quarterly e-newsletter, *iTECH DIGEST.*

Walling has written monographs; contributed articles to encyclopedias; provided pre- and post-publication book reviews; contributed chapters to various books, including scholarly history; published poems in journals and anthologies; and written several produced scripts for radio and stage as well as short story fiction. His *Arts in View* blog, which he began in 2009, is read literally around the world, as is his other blog, *Advancing Learning and Democracy,* which was launched in 2012. He was a founding associate editor of the *Journal of Gay and Lesbian Issues in Education*, now *Journal of LGBT Youth*, for which he continues to serve on the editorial board.

As a speaker, Walling has presented keynote and session presentations and workshops at international, national, regional, and state education conferences in the United States, Canada, and Germany.

Introduction

Today's students, whether in elementary school or college, are accessing knowledge differently than they did only 2 or 3 years ago. Often, information comes mainly or exclusively digitally and by using mobile devices, whether personal or supplied by their school. It makes sense that teachers need to teach differently in this new mobile digital environment. Consequently, learning designers need to approach the teaching and learning equation in new, innovative ways.

Recently a writer for *Learning Solutions Magazine* brought home the point about the mobile computing environment with some pertinent observations, namely, that in 2011 sales of smartphones topped sales of PCs and that the adoption curve for tablet computers is now predicted to climb faster than for any other mobile device, including smartphones (Poulos, 2012).

This book is about designing teaching and learning for "tablet classrooms"—that is, classrooms in which tablet computers have replaced not only students' traditional paper and pencil for a broad range of academic tasks but also laptop and desktop computers. Greater portability and lower costs when compared to desktop or laptop computers are making tablet computers a cost-effective computing choice for schools that want to move learning into the Digital Age. In ever-increasing numbers, schools are converting to tablet-mediated instruction and investing millions of dollars to purchase tablet computers for their students.

Pundits and politicians often clamor for "research-based" or "experience-based" instructional strategies and fail to understand that the road to experience begins with innovation. Innovation often requires a leap of faith—probably more than one. But the leap of innovation does not begin in thin air. Rather, the springboard is grounded by what students need to learn and how students learn best in the real world of our Digital Age. What we know about both the *what* and the *how* derive from research of a different sort.

This Digital Age shift in schools is not, or should not be, about hardware and software. It should be about teaching and learning in new and exciting ways that expand learning opportunities for *all* students—eager, capable learners and reluctant, challenged learners—at all levels, from the youngest to the most senior, and across all disciplines.

The focus of this book is instructional, or *learning*, design. It provides educators with theoretical and practical resources to capitalize on the strengths and versatility of tablet computers. It is a resource for non-techie readers written by a non-techie writer with extensive experience and expertise in innovative learning design and effective teaching. This book can also be read as an e-book, downloadable to a reading app on a tablet computer. Reading it as an e-book will provide for synchronous tablet learning. Readers can immediately apply or further investigate ideas from this book on a device already in their hands.

To make the ideas in this book maximally accessible, the tone is informal and the chapters are short. I want readers to feel as though this book is a conversation about teaching and learning—admittedly, a little one-sided. Think blog, rather than tome. I have structured each chapter to address an important consideration when planning and implementing teaching and learning mediated by computer, with particular emphasis on the tablet computer. The ideas are broadly applicable throughout the K-12 age range and into the university level as well as across the curriculum.

While I use the generic term *tablet computer*, my main point of reference is the Apple iPad. The reason is straightforward. Several manufacturers are producing tablet computers with varying degrees of success, but the iPad is the intellectual and market leader. Veteran educators will doubtless remember that Apple got its start by focusing on the education market. The first Apple computer, released back in 1976, led to the company going public in 1980. Though originally cast as a business-applications competitor for the giant IBM, Apple soon found that its most productive niche would be schools. By 1986 Apple was the market leader in school computers. That dominance has translated into today's proliferation of iPads and fully equipped "iPad classrooms," meaning a computer for every student, often expressed as 1:1 (read as "one to one").

Among the 20 chapters that follow, readers will find information about tablet computer features and functions that argue, technologically, for approaching the teaching and learning equation in unaccustomed ways. Some chapters are devoted to learning design basics tailored to the tablet computer platform, while others take up specialized topics. These topics include using e-books and eTextbooks in ways distinctly different from reading traditional paper, choosing and using software applications (apps) and Internet connectivity, capitalizing on the multisensory capabilities of tablet computers, exploring virtual worlds of learning, connecting to traditional teaching, stimulating home-school learning connections, using tablet computers for classroom management, and troubleshooting challenges that can arise in computer-mediated learning environments.

If you are reading this as an e-book, you should find that the URLs throughout are live. Clicking on them will take you to resources that expand or supplement the information within this book. Full URLs are provided if readers need to copy and paste to reach the linked resources. Of course, the usual disclaimer applies: In the ever-changing world of the Internet, the URLs were functional when this book was written, but websites do "die" or move on and so dead links are always a possibility.

Reference

Poulos, D. (2012, June 11). Mobile migration: Why your training content belongs in the cloud. *Learning Solutions Magazine*. http://www.learningsolutionsmag.com/

Chapter 1
"i" Is for Innovation

1.1 Introduction

When Apple launched the first of its "i" products, the iMac, in 1988, company officials declared that the "i" stood for "Internet" but also emphasized the company's focus on the computer as a personal device, "i" for "individual." In the context of this book, the "i" stands for "innovation"—how educators can design new approaches to teaching and learning in classrooms where students use tablet computers in place of traditional textbooks, notebooks, and other types of computers. Pundits often clamor for "experience-based" teaching strategies, but the road to experience begins with innovative learning designs grounded both in students' learning needs and the realities of their real-world experiences. Innovative teaching and learning has to take place before future teaching strategies can be "experience-based."

What are the current generation of students' realities? Today's young people have been called the "YouTube Generation," the "Net Generation," and "Generation M" (for media) for good reason. They are not only "wired" but also adept at digitally cocooning when left, literally, to their own devices. According to the *Generation M²* study (Rideout, Foehr, & Roberts, 2010), typical 8- to 18-year-olds in the United States spend nearly seven and a half hours each day using media. Because they often use two or more media at the same time, researchers estimated use to be closer to 11 hours per day, and such use did not include time spent on schoolwork using a computer or time used in talking or texting by cell phone.

This generation is defined by its use of technology, something that learning designers must take into account when planning what and how to teach. Adolescents (and even younger children) also are sometimes referred to as "screenagers." Think of the many screens they look at, the most ubiquitous being the tiny one on a cell phone or smartphone. This also applies to postadolescents, university students, and 20-somethings. The urge to use screens to create learning should be—must be—irresistible to educators. Researchers Mitzuko Ito and colleagues (2008) put it this

D.R. Walling, *Designing Learning for Tablet Classrooms: Innovations in Instruction*,
DOI 10.1007/978-3-319-02420-2_1, © Springer International Publishing Switzerland 2014

way: "Our values and norms in education, literacy, and public participation are being challenged by a shifting landscape of media and communications in which youth are central actors."

1.2 Technology Adoption Accelerates

In the 5 years between the first and second *Generation M* studies (2004 and 2009), ownership of cell phones among the 8–18 age group rose from 39 to 66 %. Access at home to high-speed wireless Internet jumped from 31 to 59 % over the same period. The pace of technology adoption, particularly among K-12 students, is approaching light speed. The pace of change in computer-related technology is already at light speed.

In 1979—ancient times by technology standards—Christopher Evans, in his landmark book, *The Micro Millennium*, described the rapid pace of computer technology change with an analogy to the automobile industry. If automobile manufacturing had developed at the same rate as computers, then today's consumers would be able "to buy a Rolls-Royce for $2.75, it would do three million miles to the gallon, and it would deliver enough power to drive the *Queen Elizabeth II*. And if you were interested in miniaturization, you could place half a dozen of them on a pinhead" (p. 76).

That was more than three decades ago. Think what is happening now.

Many adults, including educators, consider themselves to be digitally engaged, like the students in their classroom. Right? The truth is that the digital divide is not between haves and have-nots—even poor kids have cell phones—but between types of preferred digital devices across generations. Perhaps it should be called a "device divide." For example, a recent Microsoft survey posed the question, What's the best way to connect? E-mail or text message? (AARP, 2012) The results shown in Fig. 1.1 are illustrative:

E-mail is "old school," really old. But the point is that students comfortably spend hours a day focused on a handheld device that connects them to the Internet, to their friends, to their music and games, and in some cases to their other devices.

1.3 Coming of Tablet Classrooms

One perspective is to consider tablet computers as miniature laptops. In essence, laptops themselves are desktop computers that have been shrunk and made portable. That perspective mirrors the developmental history of the technology. But from the

Age	Email	Text
13 – 17	36%	64%
18 – 25	46%	62%
39 – 58	56%	40%
59 – 75	60%	19%

Fig. 1.1 Use of e-mail and text messaging by age groups

standpoint of tablet use and how educators might think about learning design that intersects with and capitalizes on students' heavy use of cell phones and smartphones, another perspective could be more helpful: Tablet computers are oversized smartphones. Think about it. The only difference is that tablets lack an actual phone, but there are lots of Internet-linked applications that offer suitable substitutes.

With the introduction of Apple's iPad tablet computer, the course of the future classroom seems set on tablet-based learning. The first-generation iPad was launched in April 2010 and sold some 300,000 units that month, 14.8 million worldwide by year's end. The fourth generation came out in November 2012, less than 3 years later. Unlike the first-generation version, the fourth-generation iPad includes a camera and a video recorder, has more versatile connectivity, and has a higher-resolution screen—and it weighs less.

A tablet market share study from November 2012 is telling. Apple's iPad accounted for 88 % of Web traffic. Its nearest competitor, Amazon's Kindle Fire, could claim only 3.6 % (Chitika, 2012). The iPad has competitors in the tablet computer field. Among them are the Samsung Galaxy, the Sony Tablet, the T-Mobile G-Slate, the Asus Transformer, the Motorola Xoom, the Toshiba Excite, the BlackBerry Playbook, the HP Slate, and the Dell Streak. Computer aficionados have their pets, but the iPad, according to most reviewers and users, stands well above the competition in most areas of functionality. The "i" in iPad really does stand for innovation; other tablet manufacturers are racing to copy and catch up.

1.4 How Tablets Are Changing Classrooms

The iPad and its competitors have already revolutionized many classrooms around the world, and more are coming online daily. Several areas are feeling the effects.

Accessibility. Tablet computers offer even greater portability than typical laptops, and their smaller size is matched by a smaller price tag, making them more affordable than traditional computers. For schools that want 1:1 computer capability for students, tablets can be a good fit for tight budgets.

Connected learning. All-iPad classrooms are proliferating to facilitate computer-mediated learning beyond the classroom. For example, in early 2012 St. Gabriel's Catholic School in Austin, Texas, unveiled a plan to issue iPads to all of its students, who will then be able to access their schoolwork both in the classroom and remotely (Hohenbrink, 2012).

Special needs. Handheld ease of use makes tablets ideal assistive devices for many learning challenges. For example, in 2011 schools in East Haven, Connecticut, spent more than $120,000 on 220 iPads to help teachers identify and help struggling readers. According to district officials, the devices allowed teachers to use time previously spent calculating and reviewing reading assessments to work with students or adjust lesson plans (Misur, 2012). Additionally, iPad classroom are not merely a phenomenon in the United States. In Australia a 7-year-old autistic youth, who used to communicate using only pictures and one or two words, is now speaking in sentences, thanks to an iPad app, according to the *Sydney Morning Herald* (Arlington, 2012).

Assessment. In the fall of 2011, the schools in Lowndes County, Alabama (2,000 students), distributed 1,100 iPads to teachers to gather observational data and to gain a glimpse of students' thought processes. In Montclair, New Jersey, at Montclair Kimberley Academy, a K-12 private school, Reshan Richards, director of educational technology says, "You can gather a lot of data quickly, and you can do a lot of quick checks of understanding in a class, but I'm more interested in the deeper, more qualitative understanding that mobile might bring" (Ash, 2012).

Textbooks. Schools also are making the move away from traditional paper to digital textbooks or eTextbooks. In March 2012, US federal officials set a goal to have a digital book in every student's hands in the next 5 years after Apple announced plans to partner with publishers to offer titles for under $15 (the program is called iBooks textbooks) and to provide a free application that makes it easy for anyone with a Mac to create a digital book. School districts in the San Diego, California, region planned to join others in the state and the country in putting high-tech tools in the hands of students to use educational apps and electronic books to augment and even replace traditional textbooks (Kucher, 2012).

1.5 Summary

The iPad (and to a lesser extent its competitors) is an international phenomenon. When the third generation was launched in March 2012, a shortage sent Russians flocking to Tokyo to get their new iPads, according to Pravda (2012). Tablet classrooms of the future are already a reality in many schools—and the numbers are rapidly rising.

Not every rollout of new technology runs smoothly, and tablets are no exception. Glitches happen—with inadequate networks, unreliable devices, unworkable policies, erroneous practices, and so forth. Articles appear periodically in the popular or education press, touting the travails of tablet experiences in schools. The press is in the bad-news business. The good news, less often reported, is about tablet classrooms that are successfully changing teaching and learning for the better in both subtle and dramatic ways.

In the chapters that follow, readers not only will be able to explore learning design strategies that can help educators and students, from kindergarten to college, take full advantage of tablet-mediated teaching and learning but also will gain insights into the kinds of applications and activities that are available to put innovative learning design into daily practice.

References

AARP. (2012). *Connecting generations*. Washington, DC: AARP Research and Strategic Analysis. http://assets.aarp.org/rgcenter/general/Connecting-Generations.pdf

Arlington, K. (2012, April 2). Speaking of useful apps, this one's a genuine life changer. *Sydney Morning Herald*. http://www.smh.com.au

Ash, K. (2012, February 8). Rethinking testing in the age of the iPad. *Education Week Digital Directions*. http://www.edweek.org

Chitika. (2012, December 6). *November tablet market share update*. Chitika Online Advertising Network. Retrieved June 24, 2013, from http://chitika.com/insights/2012/november-tablet-market-update

Evans, C. C. (1979). *The micro millennium*. New York: Viking.

Hohenbrink, M. (2012, March 3). St. Gabriel's launches 1:1 iPad initiative to flip classrooms. *T.H.E. Journal*. http://thejournal.com

Ito, M., Matteo, B., Horst, H., Bittanti, M., Boyd, D., Herr-Stephenson, B., et al. (2008). *Living and learning with new media: Summary findings from the digital youth project*. Cambridge, MA: MIT Press. http://digitalyouth.ischool.berkeley.edu/files/report/digitalyouth-WhitePaper.pdf

Kucher, K. (2012, February 27). Schools get in touch with digital books. *U-T San Diego*. http://www.utsandiego.com

Misur, S. (2012, February 12) East haven schools invest in reading technology. *New Haven Register*. http://nhregister.com

Pravda. (2012, March 16). Russians come to Tokyo for new iPads. *Pravda.ru*. http://english.pravda.ru

Rideout, V. J., Foehr, U. G., & Roberts, D. F. (2010). *Generation M^2: Media in the lives of 8- to 18-year-olds*. Menlo Park, CA: Kaiser Family Foundation. http://www.kff.org/entmedia/mh012010pkg.cfm

Chapter 2
Tablet Technology as a Moving Target

2.1 Introduction

On November 2, 1936, the British Broadcasting Corporation (BBC), operating out of the Alexandra Palace in London, began transmitting the first regular, high-definition, public television service. It is estimated that about 500 television sets would have received the first broadcast (Quick, 2009). Those few individuals who could tune in probably would have watched the BBC programs on a screen with a cathode ray tube (CRT). Screens at the time ranged from 3 to 12 in., and broadcast images were in black and white.

The innovation of television was controversial, and critics predicted both future wonders and dire consequences. Within a couple of decades, television had revolutionized society around the globe. It changed how people saw the world and themselves in it. And "the tube" profoundly affected education, altering not only what children learned but also how they learned.

On April 3, 2010, Apple revolutionized the portable computer world when the company launched the first-generation iPad. The slim, handheld computer featured a 9.7-in., full color, liquid crystal touchscreen display. Some 300,000 iPads were sold on the first day they became available (Harvey, 2010).

Today tablet technology is as controversial as early television. Enthusiastic proponents see Digital Age education propelled by tablets as a door into a new dimension previously only hinted at. More flexible than computer labs full of desktop devices and more portable than laptops, tablets offer lower costs and greater ease of use than any previous form of personal computer. Opponents, however, question whether the door to this new dimension in education ought to be opened more cautiously—or perhaps not at all.

D.R. Walling, *Designing Learning for Tablet Classrooms: Innovations in Instruction,*
DOI 10.1007/978-3-319-02420-2_2, © Springer International Publishing Switzerland 2014

2.2 Critics Weigh In

"Television won't last because people will soon get tired of staring at a plywood box every night." That was movie mogul Daryl Zanuck's opinion in 1946, and he wasn't alone (Paranicas, 2012). Every innovation, from the automobile to the computer, has been greeted with skepticism. In 1943 IBM's former chairman, Thomas Watson, predicted, "I think there is a world market for maybe five computers" (Paranicas, 2012). Of course, computers were room-filling behemoths in those days. Once size and cost came down and functionality went up, everyone wanted one. Today, around the world and across the economic spectrum, it is almost unthinkable not to own or have ready access to a computer of some sort.

When a writer poses the question, "Should kindergartners use iPads in the classroom?" and then starts a sentence, "And with the rising fad of mobile devices," the reader can be assured that the answer will be negative. Often the criticism centers on children—and, really, students of all ages—spending too much time staring at screens rather than doing other, usually more traditional learning activities. There has been a general transference of the types of criticisms that cover all sorts of screens. "In the past, we only had to be concerned about too much TV exposure," according to Mali Mann, a professor at the Stanford School of Medicine. "Now we have video games, computers, and cell phones. It is overwhelming for young children and creates patterns of behaviors similar to addiction patterns" (Rich, 2012).

This criticism is not unfounded but often is exaggerated. Teachers and parents who have used television, videos, worksheets, paper-and-pencil games, and the like to keep children occupied instead of actively engaging them in learning are likely to use, or misuse, tablets and other mobile devices in the same way. High interest and engagement can look like "addiction" without that necessarily being a negative—just the opposite, in fact. Still, the concern is not wholly unwarranted.

Nor are other criticisms completely unfounded:

- Tablet computers are an expensive experiment.
- Students will break the handheld devices, the tablets will be lost or stolen, and replacement costs will soar.
- Increasing schools' technology capabilities is too expensive.
- Students will be distracted from learning by other tablet features, such as games.

The answers to such criticisms are surprisingly straightforward.

Yes, outfitting schools with 1:1 tablet computers is expensive, but using computers in schools now has a positive track record so they are hardly an experiment. Tablets are computers with some more, some less, and some different features—and they are less expensive than laptops and desktop computers.

Yes, students will break or lose the handheld devices, but schools that have already incorporated iPads and other tablets have not found damage or loss rates in excess of normal expectations for any well-used school equipment. "We are not finding that that disaster fantasy is actually playing out in real life," according to education consultant Bernajean Porter, "including being in socioeconomic neighborhoods in which those devices might be taken from kids" (Rich, 2012). Repair and replacement costs also are lower for tablets than for laptop and desktop computers.

Yes, ramping up schools' technological infrastructure is expensive, but no matter what type of computer is used, that is a cost that will need to be paid. Computers are integral to the functioning of modern schools just as they are to other enterprises in today's world. Schools cannot remain in the twentieth century while the rest of the world functions in the twenty-first.

Furthermore, the Common Core State Standards (CCSS) that have been adopted by most of the US states include an online test component that already is pushing school districts to increase their bandwidth to accommodate mass Internet-based testing (see Quillen, 2012).

Yes, students will sometimes be distracted by tablet features, but once the novelty wears off, they are no more likely to be distracted by the tablet than they are by other, time-immemorial distractions, from birds passing the window to the irresistible urge to doodle. As a recent study concluded, "The same students who daydreamed before were still liable to wander, with or without the technology" (Upton & Konar, 2012).

Critics, from parents and kindergarten teachers to pundits and professors, are lighting their hair on fire over the proliferation of tablets in educational settings, but the panic is largely because the devices are new. They represent change, and change is always threatening to some people, including those who ought to know better.

2.3   Intuitive Integration

Early in 2013 the *Washington Post* carried a story about an experiment done by Massachusetts Institute of Technology (MIT) researchers through the One Laptop Per Child program in Ethiopia. Researchers dropped off 20 Motorola Xoom tablet computers in a small village to find out whether elementary school-age children could teach themselves to read and write in places that did not have schools and teachers. Matt Keller, director of Ethiopia's One Laptop Per Child program, said, "If we prove that kids can teach themselves how to read and then read to learn, then the world is going to look at technology as a way to change the world's poorest and most remote kids" (Associated Press, 2013).

Over the course of several months, the students not only figured out how to use the tablets but also started learning to read and write. They did so in English rather than their native Amharic because English is viewed as essential for getting better jobs. One particularly precocious 8-year-old even figured out within a few weeks how to turn on the tablet's camera, which previously had been disabled to save memory space.

The MIT experiment is only one of the many research projects being undertaken around the world to examine—and most often confirm—the value of tablet devices to improve teaching and learning.

Tablet computers at present represent a pinnacle in intuitive technology. Intensive instruction is not necessary for most users, at whatever age, to pick up a tablet device and quickly learn how to use it in basic ways. Witness the youngsters in Ethiopia. They may wear ragged clothes and live in stick-and-mud huts and they may help their parents grow potatoes and produce honey, but they intuitively can engage with a tablet computer in meaningful learning despite having no prior technology experience.

Many a parent has had the experience of their preschool child getting hold of their iPhone or iPad and later discovered that the child had downloaded a new app or played an existing game app. For many children, figuring out how to use a tablet computer may be easier than learning how to tie one's shoes or to ride a bicycle.

Therein resides the power and learning potential of tablet computers. It takes little imagination to realize how much more powerful learning might become when engaged teachers work with classrooms of students, whether kindergartners or co-eds, with tablet computers in everyone's hands.

2.4 Moving Target

Many schools have begun integration of tablet technology by providing iPads or other tablets to teachers with the idea that 1:1 student tablets would come later. This strategy is not without merit, but it can be limiting. When a teacher uses a computer to construct lesson components, this use is a step in the direction of technology-mediated learning. But simply developing traditional items such as quizzes, tests, and worksheets on a tablet does not represent a substantive change from the days when teachers ran off these paper-and-pencil components on the school's ditto machine. On the other hand, if the teachers involve students in using the computer, figuring out how to use the device together, then the potential for active learning increases. The fact is that teachers are likely to learn as much or more from their students as teachers will learn on their own.

The potential power to transform teaching and learning is more likely to be realized if dedicated student tablets arrive in conjunction with tablets for teachers. A growing number of school districts are moving in this direction—in spite of the relatively high cost and some noteworthy policy ramifications (see Chap. 14)—because the payoff in increased student learning is substantial.

In pre-tablet days, significant numbers of school districts committed to providing laptops to students and consequently discovered significant changes in how student improvement was achieved. Researcher Janet Trombley (2006), for instance, studied Project Laptop at Summit High School, an ethnically, culturally, and socioeconomically diverse public school in which students come from homes that speak 39 languages. Trombley concluded that providing computers was effective in "not only 'leveling the playing field' but also raising it by eliminating the technology disparity between the 'haves' and 'have-nots.'"

When laptop computers first came onto the market, they were the only portable computer profile available. New profiles have now emerged, including netbooks or mini-laptops; handheld devices, such as smartphones and Apple's iPod Touch; and tablet computers. Computers used to reside in separate rooms, computer labs, and one or more computers might—just might—reside in each classroom. In today's technologically rich classrooms, the teacher's dedicated computer has moved up front, supplanting the once ubiquitous chalkboard with interactive whiteboards, or IWBs, that upsize computer functionality to classroom scale. IWBs can now operate from the teacher's iPad, allowing for the sharing of a wealth of applications—from projecting traditional screen content (documents, websites, images, PowerPoint presentations) to student-produced media, such as mock senate hearings and local news broadcasts (see Chap. 17). Now, with the addition of 1:1 tablets to the electronic capacity of the classroom, new avenues of potential learning are many and ever increasing.

2.5 Summary

From the first flickering black-and-white television images nearly a century ago to the latest generation of handheld, high-definition color, touchscreen tablet computers, screens have captured the attention and imagination of generations of users of all ages. Television transformed learning, brought it home to young children in the form of *Sesame Street* and other vehicles, and took it to remote areas where TV reception existed but schools did not.

Computer technology has taken over where television left off, bringing even more changes to the way children and adults learn, both in terms of what is available to study and how they can acquire the knowledge they need and want. Tablet computers are revolutionizing the notion of what a computer is, increasing technological capabilities while downsizing scale and price. The tablets that are on the market today and those new and improved versions that will arrive tomorrow can potentially level the education playing field for students of all socioeconomic backgrounds while simultaneously expanding what and how students learn. Tablet technology is certainly a moving target, but it is one worth following.

References

Associated Press. (2013, January 18). Ethiopian kids teach themselves with tablets. *Washington Post*. Retrieved October 16, 2013, from http://www.washingtonpost.com/lifestyle/kidspost/ethiopian-kids-teach-themselves-with-tablets/2013/01/18/7f343a3a-4a1d-11e2-b6f0-e851e741d196_story.html?tid=wp_ipad
Harvey, M. (2010, April 6). iPad launch marred by technical glitches. *The Times* (UK). http://www.thetimes.co.uk/

Paranicas, P. (2012, April 5). Social media is a fad. *Flip2Market*. Retrieved October 16, 2013, from http://flip2market.com/2012/04/05/social-media-is-a-fad/

Quick, D. (2009, November 19). November 2, 1936—The beginning of television. *gizmag*. Retrieved October 16, 2013, from http://www.gizmag.com/first-bbc-television-broadcast/13397/

Quillen, I. (2012, October 15). Bandwidth demands rise as schools move to common core. *Education Week Digital Directions*. Retrieved October 16, 2013, from http://www.edweek.org/dd/articles/2012/10/17/01bandwidth.h06.html

Rich, S. (2012, May 7). Should kindergartners use iPads in the classroom? *Government Technology*. Retrieved October 16, 2013, from http://www.govtech.com/education/Should-Kindergarteners-Use-iPads-Classroom.html

Trombley, J. (2006). Project laptop: Achieving equity and access to technology in a public high school. *Integrating productivity tools in primary and secondary education*. Horizon, 2006. Retrieved October 16, 2013, from http://horizon.unc.edu/projects/monograph/K12/edited/Trombley.html

Upton, E., & Konar V. (2012). iPads and tablets in schools. *teachable.net*. http://blog.teachable.net

Chapter 3
Who's the Learning Designer Here?

3.1 Introduction

Tablet technology is still very new. Keep in mind that Apple launched the first iPad only in 2010. But already this innovation and its counterparts from other manufacturers are transforming the education landscape.

In March 2013 *Wired* magazine was able to report on a Pew study of 2,462 Advanced Placement and National Writing Project teachers, in which a reported 43 % of students had done class assignments on an iPad or other tablet computer. According to Forrester Research analyst Sarah Rotman Epps, "In the shift to digital, it's not just about replacing textbooks but inventing new ways of learning. Some of the education apps being developed for iPad are approaching learning in an entirely new way, and that's exciting" (Bonnington, 2013).

Exciting, yes. But also challenging. Applications, or apps, for the iPad and other tablet devices are proliferating at an astonishing rate. By mid-2012 the number of apps developed specifically for the iPad exceeded 225,000 (Mathis, 2012). According to the Apple website in March 2013 more than 20,000 educational apps were available in their online App Store (Apple, 2013).

The question used to be, "Who controls the curriculum: the textbook or the teacher?" Today the curriculum playing field has more players. So who does design learning? Is anyone really in charge?

3.2 The Learning Designer

Within some segments of the education profession, a transition is taking place. The term *instructional designer* is being replaced with *learning designer*. The reason behind this nominal transition is an awakening (or reawakening) notion that the focus in education should be on learner outcomes more than on instructional inputs.

D.R. Walling, *Designing Learning for Tablet Classrooms: Innovations in Instruction*,
DOI 10.1007/978-3-319-02420-2_3, © Springer International Publishing Switzerland 2014

What matters most in classrooms, proponents aver, is what students learn. Achieving desired learning outcomes must drive the *whats* and *hows* of instruction.

The term *learning designer* also is an appropriate turn of phrase because professionals who design learning contexts, environments, and activities also must be constantly learning. Static skills are inadequate in an ever-changing world. Much of the change in our world—both in the classroom and writ large—is propelled by technological change. Technological innovations and advances within education both propel and are propelled by how educators conceive learning. Consequently, learning design must be flexible not only because students are diverse in their needs, interests, aspirations, and abilities but also because the very nature of the modern world demands it. For these reasons learning designers also must be nimble adopters and adapters of technology, such as tablet computers.

Who is the learning designer? This is a simple question, but it requires a complex answer. Ultimately, the classroom teacher is the "bottom-line" learning designer. The teacher—by whatever name or title and at every level, from preschool to graduate school—is the final arbiter of factors that shape teaching and learning.

Learning design also is a partnership between teacher and learner. Instructional innovation should derive its primary impetus from students. What do they want and need to learn, why, and how can learning best be accomplished? Students, from the youngest to the most senior, learn in many different ways. An individual's "best learning mode," in fact, may not be singular but plural, depending on processing style, context, task, and other factors. Learning designers who want to be optimally effective must take all of this into account.

The goal of helping all students ultimately to become the designers of their own learning should not be merely lofty rhetoric that is unreachable in practice. Technology, with which the young seem to be almost innately adept, can provide vehicles with the power to reach just such a goal.

Twenty-first century education, however, has moved beyond the simple teacher-learner equation of Socrates or the one-room schoolhouse. Today's learning designer also must navigate some choppy bureaucratic seas, teeming with directives and influences that teachers, administrators, curriculum developers, department heads, deans, and others who would be learning designers must choose to follow, adapt, or ignore. Those influences are many and varied. Some are merely suggestive; others are authoritative, even compulsory. It is worthwhile to consider further the most important of these factors.

Three key bureaucratic (i.e., non-classroom originating) influences are curricula, standards, and tests. Whole books have been written about these factors and their effects on teaching and learning. A short summary will suffice to set the stage for the chapters that follow in this book.

3.3   Curricula

Curricula exist in many forms. There is, perhaps first of all, the internalized curriculum that every professional brings along from personal experience. It would be naïve to believe that teachers teach only as they were taught, but it would be equally naïve to ignore the influence of the personal experiences of teachers from their own days as students, from elementary school to teacher preparation classes in college.

Professional preparation has always incorporated a general sense of what teachers are expected to teacher as well as how they might go about it. These change over time, of course. And the pace of change is rapid enough that teachers still relatively new to the profession may be facing significantly different expectations than they experienced in their college classes aimed at readying them to teach. Though many people think of curriculum as mainly concerned with what is taught, the *what* is inextricably linked to the *how*. Both are constantly changing, and increasingly the *how* is mediated by technology. Effective teaching often hinges on whether change is resisted or accepted; either stance may be correct depending on the circumstances.

In the present era there is movement in the United States toward a national curriculum, at least in certain subjects. (National curricula are more common in other nations, where a national ministry for education often has greater power and influence over local education than the US Department of Education has on local American schools.) Despite its title, the Common Core State Standards (CCSS, see Refs.) define curricula in two subject areas: mathematics and English Language Arts. Although proponents claim that the development of these standards has been a "state-led" effort merely coordinated by the National Governors Association and the Council of Chief State School Officers, the standards in fact constitute a national curriculum. CCSS increase federal control of education and do so without substantially increasing federal funding. Thus, the financial burdens of implementing these curricula fall to the states and local school districts.

Curricula also are formed from state and local efforts in many subjects. A number of states have pushed back against CCSS for the very reason that they already have curricula in place with which they are satisfied. These curricula may be, or have been, developed by consortia of resident professionals, such as teachers and administrators and sometimes parents who serve on curriculum development committees at state and local levels.

Ready-made curricula also come from various sources, such as professional associations and textbook publishers. Textbook-as-curriculum is a familiar default when other curricular guidance is not available—and sometimes even when it is.

3.4 Standards

Standards generally are construed as desired, or target, competencies. They may be designated as minimal, optimal, or something in between. They are, as a rule, visionary and so likely to be more general than specific in character. A dictionary definition usually refers to a standard as a required, or at least agreed-on, level of attainment. Thus, standards are distinct from curricula. But, as the cliché goes, the devil is in the details.

When a set of related standards is developed to a high level of detail, it becomes by default a form of curriculum, which may leave little room for innovative learning design. This is essentially the problem that critics see in the Common Core State

Standards; they conflate standards with curricula. The Common Core State Standards body of required competencies is detailed to such an extent as to form national curricula for mathematics and English Language Arts, protests to the contrary aside (see, for instance, Porter-Magee & Stern, 2013).

While it may be impossible to define a precise tipping point when standards become curricula, experienced educators often discern the difference. Therein lies much of the controversy over CCSS. Overly detailed standards strip the *what* out of curriculum, leaving only the *how*.

3.5   Tests

Tests, particularly standardized, so-called high-stakes tests, can blunt learning design in much the same way as overly detailed standards. In recent decades American education has seen a proliferation of required and increasingly influential standardized tests. Many of these tests are misused—that is, used for purposes for which they were neither intended nor designed. Examples include current proposals in some states to use students' standardized test scores, at least in part, to judge teacher and school effectiveness. Such use ignores other important factors, such as socioeconomic influences that are highly correlated with student success in school and over which educators have no control. *The Myths of Standardized Tests* is aptly subtitled, *Why They Don't Tell You What You Think They Do* (Harris, Smith, & Harris, 2011). The authors parse the current mania for standardized tests, noting at the outset, "For decades more and more tests have been seeping into our schools, sapping the energy and enthusiasm of educators and draining the life from children's learning" (p. 1).

Standardized tests are not bad per se. Some are useful for diagnosis, research, and so on. But the wholesale adoption of mass standardized testing—essentially every student in every school—and the misuse of test results to judge students, teachers, schools, and entire districts is simplistic and simply wrong. Complex qualities such as student achievement, teacher quality, and school and district effectiveness cannot be reduced to a number or a set of numbers. No test score should ever constitute more than a tiny fraction of the information used to evaluate a student's learning or a teacher's effectiveness. Adding to this problem, the Common Core State Standards eventually will come with matching standardized tests to reinforce the standardization of this de facto national curriculum.

The old saw, "what gets tested is what gets taught," unfortunately can ring all too true when applied to large-scale tests that thereby narrow learning design options. My hope is that this book will help overcome some of the obstacles and limitations to effective learning design through the innovative use of tablet technology.

Note that these comments do not apply to tests that actually are integral to instruction. Classroom tests and quizzes keep testing close to learning and are beneficial because they can help shape teaching and learning. Especially helpful are self-test opportunities that allow students to shape their own learning experiences.

3.6 Technology Toolbox

The inherent hazard of classroom technology is the temptation to trade textbook-as-curriculum for technology-as-curriculum. Where once teachers debated whether students should use calculators and, if so, what kind, we now debate whether students should use computers. And, if students use computers, then what kinds of software or, in the case of tablets, apps should be permitted. Amazingly, I am old enough to have a faint memory from my elementary school days of a similar debate over whether students should be allowed to use ball-point pens in place of fountain pens. Every new device—technology—generates this debate. To use, or not to use? The question is as fraught as Hamlet's similar query.

A popular misconception is thinking of the tablet computer (or any computer) as a tool, like a ball-point pen or a calculator. It is more accurate to think of a tablet device as a whole toolbox, filled with interested and potentially useful tools. In the tablet computer classroom, apps are like individual tools. Just as wrenches and hammers are designed for different tasks, so too are apps appropriate for different types of learning in diverse circumstances.

I would argue—and hope to show in this book—that "toolbox" is perhaps too modest a concept. Perhaps "treasure chest" would be a better description. My intent is to convince readers of the tablet's value to effective learning design and, with luck and persistence, to win over those skeptics who see this treasure chest as a Pandora's box.

3.7 Summary

The partnership between teacher and student composes the foundation on which to build designs for learning. Many forces act on the teaching-learning equation, from internalized curricula and the expectations of parents, administrators, and others to the constraints of mandated curricula, standards, and high-stakes standardized tests. Not least among the powerful influences on the question, "Who is the learning designer?" is classroom technology itself, such as preprogrammed software applications, ranging from games to complex protocols. To use tablet technology effectively as a tool for teaching and learning, the learning designer must be a teacher by whatever title, who is innovative, open to change, and able to respond sensitively to the shifting teacher-student collaborations that are central to learning.

References

Apple. (2013). Apple in education. *Apple.com*. http://www.apple.com/education/ipad/
Bonnington, C. (2013, March 6). Can the iPad rescue a struggling American education system? *Wired*. Retrieved October 17, 2013, from http://www.wired.com/gadgetlab/2013/03/tablets-revolutionizing-education/

Common Core State Standards. See http://www.corestandards.org

Harris, P., Smith, B. M., & Harris, J. (2011). *The myth of standardized tests*. Lanham, MD: Rowman and Littlefield.

Mathis, J. (2012, June 11). WWDC: apple runs down the numbers. *Macworld*. Retrieved October 17, 2013, from http://www.macworld.com/article/1167183/wwdc_tim_cook_runs_down_the_numbers.html

Porter-Magee, K., & Stern S. (2013, April 3). The truth about the common core. *National Review Online*. Retrieved October 17, 2013, from http://www.nationalreview.com/articles/344519/truth-about-common-core-kathleen-porter-magee

Chapter 4
Framing the Learning Design Approach

4.1 Introduction

Designing innovative, effective learning, whether mediated by a stick drawing in the dirt or a finger drawing on the touchscreen of an iPad or other tablet computer, relies on a systematic approach to connect learners to ideas and information. Nonetheless, technology-mediated learning (TML) is different from most people's notion of traditional classroom-based education. On the whole, except in classrooms with 1:1 computers—one computer per student—where the computers are used a majority of the time, learning is not technology-mediated in the large sense. Some aspects of learning may be computer-assisted, such as when students use computers to practice skills or produce media. But 1:1 computers are not yet the norm.

On the other hand, more and more schools are adopting 1:1 computers, and tablet computers, such as the iPad, are gaining over desktop or laptop models for a variety of reasons, ranging from greater versatility to lower costs. TML requires educators to rethink how learning can be designed to capitalize on the features on offer through the tablet computer environment.

The purpose of this chapter is to provide an overview of learning theories that can help educators think in new ways about learning that capitalizes on the features of tablet technology to achieve optimal learning results.

4.2 Technology-Mediated Learning

Technology-mediated learning is a collective term, within which reside several types of technology-learning interfaces. Other terms also are descriptive, including *e-learning, networked learning, online learning, telematics, Internet learning,* and so on. Many of these terms trace their origins from the development of distance learning and concomitant technology, from early radio to today's tablet computers.

D.R. Walling, *Designing Learning for Tablet Classrooms: Innovations in Instruction,*   19
DOI 10.1007/978-3-319-02420-2_4, © Springer International Publishing Switzerland 2014

All have generated debate about precise meanings, and so it may be helpful to limit this discussion to three broad types of TML:

- *Computer-assisted* (or *aided*) *learning* (CAL) usually refers to learning situations in which the learner interacts with programmed content, sometimes in circumstances where learning in the real world is not feasible, would be prohibitively costly, or could be hazardous. Leslie Shield (2013) gives the example of learning how to operate a nuclear power plant. But Shield also points out that CAL can refer to something as straightforward as practicing a specific skill. Many tablet computer applications fit into this category of TML. CAL is a much-studied topic, and readers who want to explore CAL in depth may be interested in the Journal of Computer Assisted Learning (see Refs.).
- *Computer-mediated communication* (CMC) refers to communicative activities using computers. CMC encompasses a range of synchronous and asynchronous communications. Real-time text-conferencing and electronic, text-based chatting are examples of synchronous communication, while e-mail is asynchronous. As CMC has become more sophisticated, text-only has given way to audiovisual communication. Skype (http://www.skype.com), for example, allows computer-to-computer communication in which users see and hear one another in real time. Apple's FaceTime (http://www.apple.com/mac/facetime/) offers features similar to Skype.
- *Computer-managed instruction or learning* (CMI or CML) began to take shape during the era of early teaching machines, going back as far as the 1910s. With the advent of computers in the 1980s, CMI transitioned to the computer platform but mainly still focused on programmed instruction. CML, to use the more recent term, tends to incorporate instruction and administrative management, whether directed at a specific topic or more general in character. PLATO is an example of online courseware with a long history. PLATO (originally Programmed Logic for Automatic Teaching Operations) began at the University of Illinois in 1959 (Woolley, 1994). It is now part of Edmentum (http://www.edmentum.com).

Technology-mediated learning covers a further alphabet soup of variations and nuances related to the foregoing: learning management systems (LMS), computer-based learning (CBL), computer-assisted instruction (CAI, a variant of CAL), computer-based education (CBE), and others. The key features that coalesce under the umbrella of TML center on using the computer to:

- Engage the user in some level of learning, from basic or rote to complex and interactive
- Provide feedback to the learner using some form of response or assessment strategy, usually included in programmed learning applications
- Structure sequential learning, with the sequence in some cases determined by the learner
- Allow for management or administrative input, from recordkeeping to content manipulation

At high levels of sophistication, TML includes opportunities for interaction between learner and teacher and among learners, whether synchronous or asynchronous. This is an important development because it allows for learning designs to respond and to adapt to learner input. Unlike in the case of preprogrammed learning, which characterized early TML, the learner using interactive software applications is not required merely to march a set course but can direct that course.

Computers have made this interactive type of TML possible. Tablet classrooms place this capacity into the hands of every student. Effective learning design makes it possible to move beyond the use of programmed learning apps to engage the full spectrum of learning potential in tablet technology.

4.3   Learning Theories

All learning design proceeds from a premise that responds to the question: What is learning? Learning theories abound. Illeris (2009) in his interesting volume, *Contemporary Theories of Learning: Learning Theorists…in Their Own Words*, gathers 16 learning theories. The term *theory* is important. Illeris accurately points out that "there is no generally accepted definition" of learning. But he also suggests that "whereas learning traditionally has been understood mainly as the acquisition of knowledge and skills, today the concept covers a much larger field that includes emotional, social, and societal dimensions" (p. 1). This is a useful understanding to undergird learning design for tablet classrooms.

At the risk of oversimplification, groundwork for this book can be laid by thinking of learning theories as aggregated under three broad headings that can be juxtaposed against an understanding of technology-mediated learning:

- *Behaviorism*, which is based on observable changes in behavior, often expressed in patterns
- *Cognitivism,* which is based in the thought processes behind behavior, using observed behaviors to understand what is going on in the learner's mind
- *Constructivism,* which is grounded by the idea that learners construct understandings based on perceptions and individual experiences

Now for a bit of history. Behaviorism has long roots, going back to Aristotle, although students of learning theory are more likely to point to Russian physiologist Ivan Pavlov (1849–1936), known for his work in stimulus-response conditioning. Americans, in particular, will recognize B.F. Skinner (1904–1990) as a leading behaviorist working within education mainly in the decades surrounding the mid-twentieth century.

Most learning designers find a strictly behaviorist approach limiting. Illeris comments, for example, that behaviorism "deals with such a small corner of the vast field of learning that, in relation to human learning, it is only of interest concerning some very special fields of early learning, re-training, and certain groups of mentally handicapped learners" (p. 3). This may be a slight exaggeration. However, a certain frustration with behaviorism often is given as impetus for interest in cognitivism at mid-twentieth century.

For more information on behaviorism, readers may want to visit the website of the Association for Behavior Analysis International (ABAI) at http://www.abainternational.org. Also of interest may be an article by Henry L. Roediger (2004), titled "What Happened to Behaviorism," marking the centenary of Skinner's birth. Roediger avers that behaviorism is alive and well. He may be correct, but behaviorism offers little to inform innovative learning design for tablet classrooms because it too firmly situates control with the designer rather than the learner.

Cognitivism as a learning theory also has roots in the Ancient Greeks and can be traced to the 1920s in its modern form. The "cognitive revolution" took off in the 1960s, largely because of Swiss developmental psychologist Jean Piaget (1896–1980). There is, in fact, a Jean Piaget Society online at http://www.piaget.org. The society's quarterly journal is titled *Cognitive Development*.

Piaget is among a group of scholars who are given credit for the emergence of constructivism as a learning theory. Another historical figure is American philosopher and psychologist John Dewey (1859–1952). The term *constructivism*, however, did not figure prominently in the literature of learning theory until the 1990s.

Readers may be interested in learning more about the Association for Constructivist Teaching at https://sites.google.com/site/assocforconstructteaching/. The association publishes an e-journal titled *The Constructivist* and maintains a blog at http://constructivistblog.wordpress.com.

Learning usually is characterized by focusing on the mind, as is the case with the preceding three types of learning theory. In recent years, however, an emerging field has been *mind, brain, and education*, or MBE, which explores interactions between biological processes (brain) and learning (mind). Also referred to as *educational neuroscience*, MBE has garnered as many critics as supporters since its emergence in the 1990s. Readers may want to visit the International Mind, Brain, and Education Society website at http://www.imbes.org. The society also publishes a quarterly journal titled *Mind, Brain, and Education*.

4.4 Constructivism and Technology

In designing learning for tablet classrooms, the focusing theory in this book is constructivism. This theory, liberally interpreted from the conceptual work of scholars such as Piaget, Dewey, Lev Vygotsky (1896–1934), and Jerome Bruner (b. 1915), is extraordinarily well suited for creating challenging, productive, and engaging interconnections between the *whats* and *hows* of technology-mediated learning.

Learning designers may find it particularly useful to take a cue from Bruner's MACOS project of the 1960s. MACOS stood for Man: A Course of Study. MACOS has been updated to (Hu)man: A Course of Study and can be found online at http://www.macosonline.org.

MACOS, then and now, emphasizes learning through a cultural view of human behavior and centers around three questions:

- What makes human beings human?
- How did they get that way?
- How can they become more so?

This emphasis on the human set within culture and society is essential because the temptation to slip from technology-*mediated* to technology-*dominated* learning can be strong. Tablet apps are interesting and engaging for both children and adults, sometimes to the point of apparent addiction. In working toward innovative learning designs for tablet classrooms, it is important not to allow the tools in the tablet toolbox to take over.

The following are five observations that underpin the use of constructivist learning theory to inform technology-mediated learning design for tablet classrooms. A constructivist ethos:

- Offers multiple representations of reality
- Avoids oversimplification of real-world complexity
- Emphasizes construction rather than replication of knowledge
- Encourages reflection on what is learned and how
- Supports social and collaborative learning

As one analyst put it, tablet technology is "not just about replacing textbooks but inventing new ways of learning" (Bonnington, 2013).

4.5 Summary

As I suggested in Chap. 3, with technology as enticing as tablet computers and their wealth of available apps, the temptation is to trade textbook-as-curriculum for technology-as-curriculum. The former never was a good idea, and neither is the latter. Learning designers should not mistake the treasure chest of technology for a curriculum or, indeed, for many curricula.

A central question around which the next five chapters are framed is this: How can educators design tablet technology-mediated learning that proceeds from a constructivist point of view—that is, a philosophical and practical approach that puts direction and control of learning, to the greatest extent possible, in the hands of the learner?

References

Bonnington, C. (2013, March 6). Can the iPad rescue a struggling american education system. *Wired*. Retrieved October 17, 2013, from http://www.wired.com/gadgetlab/2013/03/tablets-revolutionizing-education/

Illeris, K. (2009). *Contemporary theories of learning: Learning theorists...in their own words*. New York: Routledge.

Journal of Computer Assisted Learning. http://onlinelibrary.wiley.com/journal/10.1111/
    (ISSN)1365-2729
Roediger, H. L (2004, March) What happened to behaviorism. *APS Observer*. Retrieved October
    17, 2013, from http://networkedblogs.com/hfwep
Shield, L. (2013) *Technology-mediated learning*. Centre for Languages, Linguistics, and Area
    Studies. Retrieved October 17, 2013, from https://www.llas.ac.uk//resources/gpg/416
Woolley, D. R. (1994, January) PLATO: The emergence of an online community. Thinkofit.com.
    Originally published in *Matrix News*. Retrieved October 17, 2013, from http://thinkofit.com/
    plato/dwplato.htm

Chapter 5
Analyzing the Learning Environment

5.1 Introduction

A BBC headline caught my attention as I was reading articles and listening to the live news stream on my iPad over breakfast on April 11, 2013. The headline read: "Global PC Sales Tumble, Data Shows." The article noted that worldwide sales of PCs fell 14 % in the first quarter of 2013. Mikako Kitagawa, a principal analyst for the market analysis firm Gartner, was quoted as saying, "Consumers are migrating content consumption from PCs to other connected devices, such as tablets and smartphones" (BBC News, 2013).

The constructivist perspective on learning design emphasizes the inclusion of "real-world complexity" (see Chap. 4). I would argue that this real-world emphasis extends not only to the subject matter to be learned but also to the technology that mediates learning.

This chapter is the first of five that will disambiguate the ADDIE approach to learning design. The letters ADDIE compose an acronym for the learning design procedural sequence: analyze, design, develop, implement, and evaluate. The ADDIE model was developed in the 1970s, originally for military purposes, but over time has been generalized to provide a useful framework for most types of learning design.

5.2 The ADDIE Model

The ADDIE instructional design model was developed at Florida State University as a way for the military to design interservice training for individuals to do specific jobs as well as for overall training curriculum development (Branson et al., 1975). Today, some 40 years later, the ADDIE model has been tinkered with and generalized to the point that it has become a generic shorthand for learning designers.

D.R. Walling, *Designing Learning for Tablet Classrooms: Innovations in Instruction*,
DOI 10.1007/978-3-319-02420-2_5, © Springer International Publishing Switzerland 2014

The phases, or steps, of the model, represented in the acronym, can be summarized as follows:

Analyze. Gather information about students (needs, abilities, prior knowledge, interests, etc.), goals for learning, settings, contexts, and technology. In short, what factors are likely to influence, either positively or negatively, the shape of the learning design?

Design. Taking into account the factors discerned during analysis, the learning designer structures a framework for learning. This phase should answer questions such as: How will learning be acquired? What are the specific learning objectives? What kinds of activities will best accomplish the objectives? How can technology be used to mediate learning?

Develop. In this phase the design blueprint of the previous phase is actualized. Resources are assembled, lessons are delineated, and sequences are ordered.

Implement. Once the learning design has been developed, it is put into service. Students engage in learning, and the learning designer or teacher makes appropriate adjustments based on interactions, observations, and formative assessments, such a quizzes and student self-tests.

Evaluate. The final phase examines the learning design to judge its success. Student learning is part of this evaluation—in other words, did students learn the intended content? However, the focus of evaluation in this phase also is on the learning design itself. Did the learning design work smoothly? Was it efficient? Effective?

Ismail Ipek and colleagues (2008), in a study of trends and approaches to learning design, comment that today's instructional design models all include steps similar to the ADDIE model but add that "recently ID [instructional design] approach is effectively combined with the field of instructional technology" (p. 515). In practice this means that, in the context of tablet classrooms, technology-mediated learning factors must permeate all of the ADDIE phases.

5.3   Phase 1: Analysis

Learning design encompasses a broad spectrum of work, and individuals in this field aggregate under various titles, such as *learning designer, instructional designer, educational technologist, curriculum designer, learning architect, learning consultant, course developer, training and development specialist, program developer and manager, instructional technologist,* and of course *teacher.* In the emerging world of the tablet classroom the teacher is likely to be a principal learning designer.

Teachers, in fact, are, or should be, frontline learning designers, although teachers' work will be influenced by other learning designers (such as curriculum directors) and increasingly by would-be instructional designers (such as politicians and policy makers).

It is not an infrequent scenario as schools and districts implement 1:1 tablet technology for teachers to arrive in their classrooms on the opening day of school to find not only a sea of fresh-faced students but also a cartload of tablet computers, often with little prior training or practice with the new devices. So…what comes next?

In an ideal education environment, of course, teachers would have adequate training prior to being thrown into a tablet classroom. Most often this ideal is not realized, and training is sketchy at best. Consequently, effective teachers draw on both art and science to craft teaching and learning for their students, whether collectively or individually. If we compare effective teachers to jazz musicians, they must be exemplary players, more than merely technically competent. They know when to follow the score (the curriculum) and when to improvise. Teachers who aspire to be exemplary learning designers, especially in tablet classrooms, must be virtuosos.

To put learning design into a relevant context from outside the classroom, let's consider someone who works professionally in the field. Michael Shermis (2013) is a virtuoso learning designer. He is president of the consulting firm Story Insights (http://storyinsights.com) in Bloomington, Indiana. Shermis describes himself as a *story developer,* rather than a *learning designer*, but his company provides a variety of services, including learning design. His experience includes nearly 20 years of consulting with enterprises ranging from local nonprofits to international Fortune 500 companies.

According to Shermis, "A story is…about developing a mission, a vision, values, strategies, and much more." He explains, "Starting with what you do and where you want to be, your vision, and how you're going to try to get there and how you're going to treat people—you're developing a story. As I tell my clients, the people in the organization: You're the characters in the story. And it involves learning design all along the way."

How does that translate into designing learning for tablet classrooms? One approach, suggested by Shermis' story perspective, is for teachers to frame classroom learning design as the development of students' individual and collective stories.

A story turns on solving problems, according to Shermis. "A problem of some sort is at the heart of any story. How to solve the problem or problems is the lesson. The context makes it important to the learner, who wants to be successful." Shermis concludes by saying, "It begins with a lot of questions."

Isn't that true for any analysis? Michael Shermis' approach to learning design merges art and science to contextualize learning and make it real. Whether readers use this story framework or some other approach to learning design, the essentials of analysis as a first step are the same.

5.4 Using OPUS for Analysis

At the risk of adding yet another acronym to the alphabet soup that characterizes education lingo, I will nonetheless suggest OPUS as a mnemonic for observe, probe, unify, and stage. These four processes compose a useful, systematic, and relatively simple way to analyze the elements that every teacher must take into account when designing learning. Earlier I compared teachers to jazz virtuosos. In music, as in literature (Shermis' story?), an opus is a creative work, often of special significance. Consequently, the acronym OPUS is appropriate for approaching an essential phase in the creation of effective learning designs for tablet classrooms. The acronym can be parsed as follows:

Observe. Any analysis of teaching and learning should begin with observation. It is easy to get off on the wrong foot when a teacher or other learning designer simply plunges in without taking time to see—really see—how students respond to topics and technology. In tablet classrooms it is equally important to observe both how students respond to subject matter and how they interact with devices. The former type of observation should be standard; the latter may be new to teachers and students just getting started in 1:1 tablet environments.

Many of today's students, even quite young ones, will be familiar with tablets or tablet-like devices. It's not unusual for parents and toddlers to play games, listen to music, or look at pictures and videos on handheld devices such as smartphones, iPods, and so on. Kindles, Nooks, and other e-readers provide a wealth of children's literature and have features similar to those found on tablet computers. From lap time onward, many children gain increasing familiarity and ease with handheld devices.

Even when students come into the tablet classroom with no prior device experience, it seldom takes long for them to become curious, first, and then adept at manipulating the basic features of tablets. Recall the account mentioned in Chap. 2 about the Ethiopian children who taught themselves to use tablet computers without any adult intervention (Associated Press, 2013). The point is that teachers should observe students carefully to gauge not only content knowledge and interest but also interest and knowledge of the technology.

Probe. Observation is followed or coupled with probing for information. Most teachers have at their command a number of strategies for getting at and then activating their students' prior knowledge of content or skills. Probing usually centers on asking questions. One framework is KWL, which is a mnemonic for: What do students *know*? What do students *want* to learn? And later, What have students *learned*? It is usually more helpful to ask questions about what is important to future learning, rather than what is unusual or different. Often it can be as simple as "What do you know about…?" or "What can you tell me about…?"

A similar approach is useful when probing students' technological knowledge. Do students know simple functions, such as how to turn on the device, how to use gestural screen commands, how to open an app, how to bring up the keyboard, and so forth? Probing to understand how well students can use a tablet device can be couched in demonstration terms: "Can you show me how to…?" Probing can be done with individuals, small groups, or whole classes. This is an important step in analyzing the teaching and learning situation before making learning design decisions.

Unify. Observing and probing provide information that can compose a holistic approach to learning design. This information should lead to more than merely a starting point. For example, if the teacher observes that students do not know how to open a note-taking app, bring up the keyboard, key in text, and save what they have done to come back to later, then the framework of the learning design will need to be constructed toward a technological literacy goal, namely, how to use a note-taking app. On the other hand, if observing and probing reveal that students know how to manipulate an app about, say, doing basic algebra, then the framework of the learning design can be constructed toward a goal of using the app and integrating tablet-based lessons with group and individual classroom activities to increase content knowledge and skills in algebra.

The idea behind unifying as an analytical step is that a goal, or endpoint, in a learning design is implicit in the starting point. Effective learning design can be best accomplished through well organized—in other words, unified—lesson components, rather than vague, sweeping concepts or worse, large-scale, overly detailed, preprogrammed approaches that ignore the day-to-day classroom realities of teaching and learning.

Stage. To stage learning design during the analysis phase of the ADDIE model means to begin consideration of how teaching and learning might proceed in an orderly manner. Staging will be further refined in later ADDIE phases. The intent at this point is simply to initiate thinking about how a learning design that incorporates designated subject matter and tablet technology might be ordered.

From a constructivist viewpoint, the gradual release of responsibility model offers a helpful concept. The model's principles are straightforward and hardly unique, but the model name is attributed to P. David Pearson and Margaret C. Gallagher (1983). The model contains essentially four steps:

- Modeling—"I do, you watch"
- Sharing—"I do, you help"
- Guiding—"You do, I help"
- Applying—"You do, I watch"

These steps are sometimes given other labels. For example, they might be *demonstration, guided practice, independent practice,* and *application.* The point is that the teacher gradually relinquishes control of learning as students assume control and self-direction. The staging phase of analysis offers an opportunity to consider how the learning design might be constructed to foster student investment and involvement in learning and, ultimately, independence.

5.5 Summary

Predominantly constructivist approaches to learning design emphasize real-world complexities, and those complexities include the use of computer technology not only "out there" but in schools and individual classrooms. One-to-one tablet technology offers new opportunities for students to engage in technology-mediated learning that are more personal, more individualized than was possible in the computer lab and shared computer school environments.

The ADDIE approach to learning design is adaptable to virtually any classroom situation, subject matter, and age/grade level. The *A* in the acronym—analysis—encompasses both art and science as the learning designer examines content, processes, and technology. Call it developing a "story," as Michael Shermis does, or use another term. The result is the same: a first step toward developing an effective design for learning.

Within analysis, use of the OPUS strategy frames a systematic approach. By incorporating observation, probing, unifying, and staging, the teacher can reasonably ensure a thorough analysis on which to base the learning design.

References

Associated Press. (2013, January 18). Ethiopian kids teach themselves with tablets. *Washington Post*. http://www.washingtonpost.com/lifestyle/kidspost/ethiopian-kids-teach-themselves-with-tablets/2013/01/18/7f343a3a-4a1d-11e2-b6f0-e851e741d196_story.html?tid=wp_ipad

BBC News. (2013, April 11). Global PC sales tumble, data shows. *BBC News*. Retrieved from iPad BBC News app; also available from http://www.bbc.co.uk/news/business-22103079

Branson, R. K., Rayner, G. T., Cox, J. L., Furman J. P., King, F. J., & Hannum W. H. (1975, August). *Interservice procedures for instructional systems development*. (5 vols.) (TRADOC Pam 350-30 NAVEDTRA 106A). Ft. Monroe, Va.: U.S. Army Training and Doctrine Command. (NTIS No. ADA 019 486 through ADA 019 490)

Ipek, I., Izciler, M., & Baturay M. H. (2008). New trends and approaches in instructional design and technology: From schools to industry. In *Proceedings of the 8th International Educational Technology Conference* (pp. 508–512). Eskişehir, Turkey: Anadolu University

Pearson, P. D., & Gallagher, M. C. (1983). The instruction of reading comprehension. *Contemporary Educational Psychology, 8*, 317–344.

Shermis, M. (2013, March 6). (president, Story Insights), in discussion with the author.

Chapter 6
Designing Learning That Capitalizes on Tablet Technology

6.1 Introduction

ADDIE is the acronym for a five-step approach to learning design. The initials stand for analyze, design, develop, implement, and evaluate. Overlaying this model is a constructivist orientation that focuses instruction on the learner rather than the teacher.

While much of the information in this book is applicable to learning design at various levels, the main focus is on classroom teachers in tablet classrooms—that is, classrooms in which students, regardless of age or grade level, use tablet computers. In 1:1 tablet classrooms, each student has an iPad or other tablet computer. A central feature of tablet classrooms is that students use tablets in place of traditional textbooks, pencil and paper, and other types of computers.

In Chapter 5 the topic was *A*, for analysis. In this chapter I take up the first *D*: design. How should learning be designed based on the analysis done in the first phase of the ADDIE model to incorporate effective use of tablet technology?

6.2 Phase 2: Design

In the previous chapter I suggested that using an OPUS approach to analysis could be beneficial. This acronym stands for observe, probe, unify, and stage. These four processes can systematically inform the design for learning. The fourth of these— stage—refers to initiating consideration of how teaching and learning might proceed in some orderly manner. The second ADDIE phase—design—is about creating that order in full.

In connection with the stage step of the OPUS approach, I also referred to the gradual release of responsibility model as a way of approaching learning design from a constructivist perspective, one that is student-centered and moves learning from being teacher-controlled and teacher-focused to student-controlled and student-focused

D.R. Walling, *Designing Learning for Tablet Classrooms: Innovations in Instruction*, DOI 10.1007/978-3-319-02420-2_6, © Springer International Publishing Switzerland 2014

(Pearson & Gallagher, 1983). To reiterate, the gradual release of responsibility model in its ideal form follows a four-part sequence that goes something like this:

- Modeling—"I do, you watch"
- Sharing—"I do, you help"
- Guiding—"You do, I help"
- Applying—"You do, I watch"

Taking into account the factors discerned during analysis, the learning designer's challenge is to bring together this wealth of information, interfacing it with goals, objectives, and other expected outcomes that may be part of the teacher's personal agenda, required by policy from one or more administrative levels, or, more likely, some combination of these influences. The design phase should answer:

- How will learning be acquired?
- What are the specific learning objectives?
- What kinds of activities will best accomplish the objectives?
- How can technology be used to mediate the desired learning?

As these questions are confronted, the answers are likely to give rise to additional questions, depending on the nature of the subject matter, characteristics of students, the learning environment, and other factors. For the purpose of this book, the final question above, regarding technology, will be the focus.

6.3   To Tablet or Not to Tablet

To borrow from Shakespeare, I suggest that the learning designer's question ought to put a spin on one asked by Hamlet: To tablet or not to tablet? When does technology facilitate learning and when does it get in the way or just not help? Multimodal teaching is essential—perhaps even more so in technologically rich classrooms, where teachers may feel pressured to overuse technology when other methods may, in fact, be more appropriate.

A decision matrix can be useful for delineating aspects of a learning sequence for which tablet technology may be unnecessary, helpful, or essential. The template illustrated in Fig. 6.1 includes learning objectives, technology specifics, and anticipated outcomes. It can easily be expanded or integrated into an existing lesson planning protocol.

As an example, let's consider a middle or high school literature lesson about Mark Twain. Assume that the lesson comes midyear and that the analysis phase has discovered that students have some basic knowledge. They know Twain was an American author who wrote short stories and novels. Now the teacher wants to explore Twain's nonfiction. Let's also assume that students are familiar with basic functions on their tablets, such as searching the Internet. What are some activities that might foster learning about Twain's nonfiction, and how might tablet technology be used? Or should it be used?

Learning Objective(s):				
Activities	Technology Mediation U – H – E*	Type of Technology Needed	Strategies	
Anticipated Outcome(s):				

*Unnecessary, Helpful, Essential

Fig. 6.1 Technology-mediation decision matrix

One activity might be to begin by asking students to find out whether Twain wrote any nonfiction and, if so, what are some examples. Would tablet technology be unnecessary, helpful, or essential to this activity? That answer could well depend on certain circumstances. For instance, are traditional resources, such as an encyclopedia or a biography of Twain, available to answer the initial question? If they are, then technology might be deemed unnecessary. But depending on the extent of the traditional resources, the technology could just as easily be seen as helpful. An Internet search on, say, "Mark Twain nonfiction" probably would turn up more resources than are ready to hand in most schools.

A recent examination of library services in the Digital Age by the Pew Research Center found that even when traditional library resources are abundant, 66 % of patrons age 16 and older who used computers in a library did research for school or work (Zickuhr, Rainie, & Purcell, 2013).

Consider a different scenario: a technology-based school. Nontraditional, high-tech schools are proliferating that do not have libraries and other print resources usually associated with traditional schools. Such schools are computer dependent; their libraries are online. Take this scenario a step further: virtual classes. These are classes or entire schools that exist partially or wholly online. In these scenarios, tablet technology (or some form of connected computer technology) is essential to answer the question about Twain and nonfiction.

Another activity in this lesson might be to locate a nonfiction work by Twain, read all or a portion (perhaps a full essay or a chapter in a book), and then summarize the text. The same considerations apply. Depending on the physical resources available, tablet technology may be unnecessary or merely helpful. But it could, in fact, be essential. Let's assume, for instance, that the school library (if there is one) does not include any of Twain's nonfiction in its collection. An Internet search will locate The Literature Network webpage about Mark Twain at http://www.online-literature.com/twain/, where students will find a list of Twain's publications categorized under fiction, nonfiction, short stories, essays, and poetry. All of the listed resources link to freely available text. For instance, if the student chooses Twain's 1880 account of his European travels, *A Tramp Abroad*, the site will offer chapter-by-chapter links. Click on any chapter link and read.

The Literature Network is a commercial website, and this raises some other considerations. For one thing, the site is full of ads, which seem intrusive and annoying. Some users will find this a small price to pay for such a wealth of free content, which includes not only the literary text but also summaries of works, author information, and other teacher-friendly features, at least for certain works. The ads can be eliminated by subscribing to the site and paying a fee. The fee structure accommodates individuals, teachers and students, libraries, and school districts for various lengths of time. Subscription also adds some management tools for teachers.

Any use of the Internet comes with pluses and pitfalls, a topic taken up in more depth in Chap. 14. Taking into account these concerns, such as whether to use a commercial website, is part of designing the learning experience.

As an alternative to The Literature Network, a teacher might ask students to use an app called Free Books (for iPad at https://itunes.apple.com/us/app/free-books-23-469-classics/id364612911?mt=8) and download *A Tramp Abroad* or one of the other available works by Twain to read as a free e-book. Similar apps are available for other platforms. This approach to accessing text is different from the one offered on the commercial website, but it is a judgment call whether it is more or less desirable as a lesson component.

The point is that availability is an important consideration. A wealth of older—in other words, out of copyright—literature is freely available on the Internet. Contemporary literature is another matter. Asking students to locate, download, and read works by living writers or even authors who published within the last 75 years may be unreasonable, as some costs will almost certainly be involved. Obscure works, which can be difficult to locate in physical form, may never have been digitized. This latter concern may not matter except in graduate-level settings. The former will be an issue in any subject area where contemporary documents are needed. However, it is important to remember that cost and availability issues will arise regardless whether the materials are obtained in physical or digital form.

6.4 Networking Considerations

Beyond considerations of how basic tablet features and Internet connectivity can facilitate learning design are questions that revolve around types of networking. These questions can be grouped into two categories: personal and classroom. (School and district networking questions more often concern management issues than teaching and learning.)

Let's continue with the hypothetical lesson about Mark Twain's nonfiction. As students read their chosen selections, they will need to take notes that will later be the basis of individual reports. A student might take notes using paper and pencil, making tablet technology unnecessary. But advantages may be gained by using a note-taking app, including being able to tap into an individualized, personal electronic network using cloud computing.

Cloud computing uses remote, or Internet-based, resources such as servers and storage to connect, or network, user services. For example, if the student uses a note-taking app such as Evernote (https://evernote.com), then cloud computing will allow the student's notes to be accessed on any device equipped with that app.

As I write this chapter, we are hosting an exchange student from Germany, an eleventh-grader who moves casually and confidently among several devices. It is not unusual for him to begin a school report on his laptop at home, continue writing "on the go" using an iPod Touch, and then finish the report on a device at school. Cloud computing allows him to upload text or other types of files (photos, videos, music) from any device and retrieve them on other devices.

At the classroom level, the use of a classroom cloud can facilitate the sharing of files among students and teachers. For example, all of the students' reports on their explorations of Twain's nonfiction can be uploaded so that other students and the teacher can access the reports. In tablet classrooms, uploading schoolwork to the classroom cloud can replace the physical act of turning in assignments on paper.

Use of cloud computing is spreading. In *Silver Linings and Surprises*, the 2013 State of the Cloud Report from the technology provider CDW (http://www.cdw.com), researchers looked at cloud computing adoption by schools. Among the findings, they noted that:

- 76 % of IT professionals in K-12 schools acknowledged that their use of the cloud at home has influenced their recommendations at work about moving to the cloud.
- 56 % of IT professionals believe school employees' personal use of cloud applications or mobile devices is making their school move faster to the cloud.
- 42 % of K-12 schools are implementing or maintaining cloud computing, up from 27 % in 2011 (CDW, 2013).

Many students are already making personal use of cloud computing, as are many teachers. A natural evolution of such use is the expansion to classroom clouds. Consequently, networking at personal and classroom levels should be considered in designing effective learning.

6.5 Summary

Cloud computing moves tablet technology beyond the device itself. It is possible, of course, to use an unconnected tablet—that is, to use only apps that have been installed and do not require Internet connectivity to function. However, such use is hardly optimal. Tablet computers should not be merely expensive paper substitutes. Internet connectivity expands tablet functionality exponentially. Students and teachers who connect to the Internet can access information literally from around the world and across the ages. Add the dimension of cloud computing and students and teachers can expand how they share information. Instead of merely exchanging papers physically with their classmates or turning in assignments to their teachers, students can share texts, photographs, videos, and other information not only with their classmates but also potentially with counterparts anywhere in the world.

Many observers have noted that students of all ages tend to be early adopters of new technology. The 3-year-old who is downloading game apps on her mother's smartphone today will come to school in a few years fully able to capitalize immediately and with little instruction on the features of tablet technology. He or she also will come with an expectation that technology will be integral to learning, as indeed it should be. Tablet technology can help teachers move rapidly and seamlessly from "I do, you watch" to "You do, I watch."

References

CDW. (2013, Author). *Silver linings and surprises*. (CDW's 2013 State of the Cloud Report). http://www.cdw.com

Pearson, P. D., & Gallagher, M. C. (1983). The instruction of reading comprehension. *Contemporary Educational Psychology, 8*, 317–344.

Zickuhr, K., Rainie, L., & Purcell, K. (2013, January 22). Library services in the digital age. Pew Internet and American Life Project. Retrieved October 20, 2013, from http://libraries.pewinternet.org/2013/01/22/library-services/

Chapter 7
Developing Activities That Match Learning Needs

7.1 Introduction

Tablet computer technology offers a wide variety of applications, from self-contained software to Internet-based programs. In considering the second *D*—development— of the ADDIE model for learning design, several questions arise. How should teachers choose appropriate technological mediation? What are reasonable criteria? And when should teachers avoid preprogrammed activities in favor of developing mixed (traditional and technological) or adapted technology-mediated learning activities? How can tablet technology assist in designing learning that engages students individually, cooperatively, or collaboratively as best suits the situation?

Many preprogrammed apps on tablets offer simple behaviorist-style instruction— stimulus-response, if you will. Do a certain procedure and *x* predictably results. Such apps may be appropriate for basic skills practice, but they neither permit nor encourage higher-level thinking, such as the construction of complex meaning. The challenge for the learning designer is not to limit tablet technology use to simplistic, behaviorist functions but to develop ways to employ tablet technology in sophisticated, interactive, constructivist learning strategies.

7.2 Phase 3: Development

A predominantly constructivist orientation toward the development phase of the ADDIE model draws on a wealth of student-centered learning and development theories, including those of Jean Piaget (1896–1980) and Urie Bronfenbrenner (1917–2005). Bronfenbrenner used the term *ecology* to encompass the notion that human development occurs and is shaped within the context of a person's surrounding influences.

The following are brief descriptions of each of these theorists' central ideas. These summaries risk a disservice to both theorists, as their work and that of others who have built on their ideas have filled volumes. However, these concise synopses are intended merely to sketch a guide for the suggestions in this chapter about developing designs for learning specifically for tablet classrooms.

Cognitive Development Theory. Piaget observed that as children mature they acquire knowledge and understanding according to their own mental structures. These structures are malleable. As learners interact with changing surroundings, they modify their mental structures to meet the demands of the environment. For example, infants initially engage mainly in reflex actions, such as sucking. As they mature they pick up objects and put them in their mouths. But not all objects are subject to reflex actions, and so they must adapt their responses. Piaget believed that the tension between reflex and accommodation stimulated intellectual growth or learning (Ormrod, 2012).

Piaget articulated four stages of cognitive development:

- *Sensorimotor*—Birth to age two
- *Preoperational*—Age two to seven
- *Concrete Operational*—Age 7–11
- *Formal Operational*—Adolescence to adulthood

Kay C. Wood and her colleagues (2001) note that researchers in the 1960s and the 1970s found problems with the lack of flexibility in Piaget's stages. Children's and adolescents' thinking is more diverse and task-dependent than would be expected in a strict interpretation of this cognitive model.

For example, moving from concrete to abstract thinking is key to understanding algebra, with which many students struggle, particularly at younger ages when they theoretically are in Piaget's concrete operational stage. However, Henry Borenson's work with young children using his Hands-On Equations program (available as a series of apps as well as in physical, individual, and classroom-scale programs—see http://www.borenson.com) demonstrates that if children experience algebraic principles using concrete strategies initially, then the transition to abstract thinking can occur at younger ages (Borenson & Barber, 2008).

Overlaying flexibility on the Piagetian stages moves this view of learning along the continuum from cognitivism to constructivism.

Ecological Systems Theory. Bronfenbrenner asserted that a person's cognitive development reflects the influence of various environmental systems or ecologies (Bronfenbrenner, 1979). He delineated these systems as follows:

- *Microsystem* refers to institutions and groups that have most directly affected a child's development, such as family, neighborhood, school, and peers.
- *Mesosystem* refers to relationships between microsystems, such as how family experiences relate to school experiences.
- *Exosystem* refers to connections between individuals and social settings in which they have no role, such as how a child's home experience is affected by his or her mother's work experience.
- *Macrosystem* refers to the larger culture of the individual. Cultural contexts include socioeconomic status and ethnicity, for example. Bronfenbrenner believed that macrosystems evolve because of changes in succeeding generations.

- *Chronosystem* refers to environmental events and transitions over time. For example, divorce affects many children in school, but the negative effects tend to peak early and then level out after the first year or so.

Bronfenbrenner also acknowledged that individuals bring biological and genetic aspects into the equation, later referring to ecological systems theory as "bioecological" (Bronfenbrenner, 2005). "He devoted more attention, however, to the personal characteristics that individuals bring with them into any social situation," according to researcher Jonathan Tudge and his colleagues (2009, p. 200).

Some critics contrast the developmental theories of Piaget and Bronfenbrenner, viewing the former as intrapersonal and the latter as interpersonal. Certainly there are distinctions to be made between cognitivists and constructivists. However, Piaget espoused a child-centered approach to teaching and learning, saying, "Education means making creators…inventors, innovators—not conformists" (Bringuier, 1980, p. 132). He believed that children developed best through interaction, which is consistent with the largely constructivist approach to learning design described in this book, particularly when Piaget's stages of cognitive development are viewed as general and flexible, rather than specific and static.

Jerome Bruner, discussed earlier (see Chap. 4), falls into the interpersonal, social/cultural-context frame of reference, along with Lev Vygotsky and others. However, the threads of commonality between the development theories of Piaget, Bronfenbrenner, and their respective followers, for all practical purposes, are stronger than the contrasts. And practical purposes are the focus of this book.

7.3   A Cognitive-Ecological Approach

Students at all ages interact with technology outside the classroom as well as inside. Even the youngest pupils now very often come to school already knowing how to use the basic functions of tablet-style devices, such as iPods and smartphones. With older students some schools employ BYOD, or bring-your-own-device, strategies. (More about this BYOD in Chaps. 17 and 18.) Device distinctions aside, once teachers and students have a common frame of reference with regard to the available technology, more important learning questions can be posed to refine the design framework constructed in the previous chapter.

The following are suggestions to guide development of the learning design. This development phase is used to flesh out the various considerations that may have been summarized using the technology-mediation decision matrix shown in Fig. 6.1. Perhaps it's my early newspaper training, but I find that the journalist's standard five W's and H questions are helpful to guide thinking about development. (For non-journalists, the questions ask who, what, when, where, why, and how.)

Who will learn? This consideration goes beyond simply whether students are younger or older, concrete thinkers, or abstract thinkers. The question comes down to individual learning styles and group dynamics. Some students work more effectively on certain tasks when they are allowed to do it alone. Others need peer support and

Fig. 7.1 Bloom's taxonomy

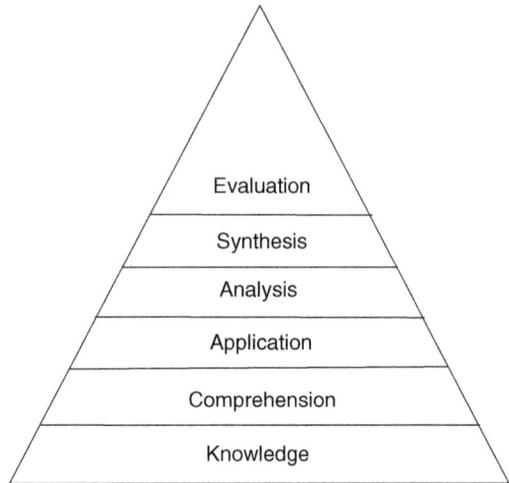

work best in teams, triads, or small groups. And some learning objectives simply are most effectively attained using whole-class instruction. Not only the students themselves but also the learning tasks will guide the answers to these questions, and thus the answers will guide decisions about technology, both at the macro level (whether to use tablet technology) and the micro level (which apps to use).

What will they learn? Does the learning design call for acquiring basic knowledge or skills, or is higher-order thinking the goal? Although Benjamin Bloom's taxonomy of the cognitive domain has been tinkered with and revised multiple times, I prefer the original categories for thinking about a hierarchy of knowledge acquisition (Bloom, Engelhart, Furst, Hill, & Krathwohl, 1956). Figure 7.1 provides the standard illustration of Bloom's taxonomy. The nature of the learning topic and the level of intellectual development of the students cross-referenced with the level of desired learning will guide choices of mediating technology. Among the multitude of available tablet apps are those that function at one or more of the six taxonomy levels, from simple skills-practice apps to fully interactive apps that require integrative thinking and judgment.

When will they learn? Timing is a critical, though sometimes undervalued, consideration within an ecological framework. The learning objective and the activities sketched in the technology-mediation decision matrix provide a starting point. Will learning be accomplished as a start-up (start of day, start of class, start of week) or a closer (end of day, class, or week)? Will the activities be accomplished in a single time frame, or will lessons extend over several days or weeks? Shorter designs tend to be more manageable—as well as easier to adapt to changing circumstances, such as students taking more or less time than anticipated to master certain concepts or acquire designated skills. Complex learning objectives often are better divided among several sub-objectives.

Where will they learn? This is another important ecological consideration. Will the learning objectives be accomplished in the classroom, a lab setting, at home, on a field trip, indoors or outdoors, or in a virtual setting? Surroundings can establish not only the overall learning environment but also dictate what tools and resources are available. With some forms of technology, virtual settings are an added consideration. For example, frog dissection once was a standard lesson in tenth-grade biology. Generations of adults still remember the formaldehyde fumes and the exclamations of "Ewww!" that accompanied that lesson. Today, if schools have limited lab facilities, face ethical dilemmas about physical dissection, or simply have students who are squeamish about cutting open preserved frog specimens, there are apps for virtual frog dissection (see, e.g., http://www.frogvirtualdissection.com). (Chapter 16 discusses other real-versus-virtual considerations.)

Why will they learn? The elaboration of a learning design and its placement within the overall curriculum will depend on why the learning objectives have been included in the instructional scope and sequence. Does the learning design focus on foundational, must-have knowledge and skills—things that must be mastered in order to move forward? Do the objectives represent a capstone, a bringing together of ideas and information learned over time? Are the learning objectives integral to the adopted standards or required curricula, or are they supplemental, such as for adaptive or enrichment purposes? These are prioritization questions. How they are answered also may affect choices of technology mediation.

How will they learn? Is technology useful, helpful, or essential? An indication of this question is included in the technology-mediation decision matrix. But this question also reiterates one of the *who* considerations above: Will students benefit most from learning on their own or with others? If with others, in small groups or whole class? Will they share technology in some way—two students/one device or students electronically linked on individual devices? The sharing question is obvious when considering learning games, but it also is applicable when working on group reports or other tasks in which students work together on a common goal or project.

It should be borne in mind that how some of these questions are answered also may depend on whether Internet connectivity is available. A reminder of the importance of considering this factor came in the form of an e-mail from a colleague in Florida, elementary special needs educator Connie Huston, who has been piloting iPads with her students. "Fifth-graders were doing state testing for the first time in our computer lab, and the district put out a ban on any other students/teachers using computers or iPads," she wrote. "I was bemoaning what a drastic change this would be for my class. Then the computer tech from the district said we could just disable Internet connectivity and use apps only" (Huston, 2013).

Tablets or no tablets, connectivity or not—availability is a key consideration. The effect of limited broadband capacity—the number of users who can be online simultaneously—as districts ramp up to accommodate increased use of the Internet may require teachers to find, as Connie Huston did, work-around solutions to carry out their learning designs. (For a fuller discussion of systemic—e.g., connectivity—challenges, see Chap. 20.)

7.4 Summary

In developing a learning design, tablet technology offers a range of applications. Whether to employ technology is the first question. If the answer is affirmative, then the development questions in this chapter aim at refining how best to use the tablet "toolbox" and the app "tools" within it. From a constructivist viewpoint, the more effectively technological tools can be used to move teachers and students from "I do, you watch" to "You do, I watch" in which students "own" their own learning, the better.

The cognitive-ecological approach suggested in this chapter draws on time-tested strategies to assist in developing the learning design. The journalist's five W's and H are cross-referenced with Bloom's traditional taxonomy of the cognitive domain. In furthering the constructivist orientation, clearly a concomitant goal is to move students from basic to higher-level thinking. The questions in this chapter point toward straightforward strategies that all teachers can use, regardless of subject matter or students' intellectual maturity, to develop an effective learning design.

References

Bloom, B. S., Engelhart, M. D., Furst, E. J., Hill, W. H., & Krathwohl, D. R. (Eds.). (1956). *Taxonomy of educational objectives—The classification of educational goals—Handbook 1: Cognitive domain*. London, WI: Longmans, Green & Co.

Borenson, H., & Barber, L. (2008, March 17). The effect of Hands-On Equations® on the learning of algebra by 4th and 5th graders of the Broward County Public Schools. Retrieved April 27, 2013, from http://www.borenson.com/

Bringuier, J.-P. (1980). *Conversations with Jean Piaget*. Trans. B.M. Gulati. Chicago: University of Chicago Press.

Bronfenbrenner, U. (1979). *The ecology of human development: Experiments in nature and design*. Cambridge, MA: Harvard University Press.

Bronfenbrenner, U. (2005). The biological theory of human development. In U. Bronfenbrenner (Ed.), *Making human beings human: Bioecological perspectives on human development* (pp. 3–15). Thousand Oaks, CA: Sage.

Huston, C. (2013, April 28). (elementary special needs teacher), in discussion with the author.

Ormrod, J. E. (2012). *Essentials of educational psychology: Big ideas guide to effective teaching*. Boston, MA: Pearson.

Tudge, J. R. H., Mokrova, I., Hatfield, B. E., & Karnik, R. B. (2009). Uses and misuses of Bronfenbrenner bioecological theory of human development. *Journal of Family Theory and Review, 1*, 198–210.

Wood, K. C., Smith, H., & Grossniklaus D. (2001). Piaget's stages of cognitive development. In M. Orey, ed. *Emerging perspectives on learning, teaching, and technology*. Athens, GA: University of Georgia, College of Education. Retrieved April 27, 2013, from http://www.coe.uga.edu/epltt/

Chapter 8
Implementing the Learning Design

8.1 Introduction

Chapter 6 introduced the acronym OPUS—for observe, probe, unify, and stage—as a mnemonic for four critical processes that inform a learning design. When approaching learning design from a constructivist orientation, staging refers to ordering learning experiences in a way that implements the gradual release of responsibility model. This model, as noted earlier, follows a four-part sequence according to Pearson and Gallagher (1983):

- Modeling—"I do, you watch"
- Sharing—"I do, you help"
- Guiding—"You do, I help"
- Applying—"You do, I watch"

The *I* in the ADDIE model stands for *implementation*. In considering how lessons should unfold during the implementation phase, the central question is: What roles should teachers take? The plural, roles, is intentional. While there is an implicit order in the gradual release of responsibility, all four stages are not always needed in every lesson. For instance, if students are already familiar with the broad outlines of a topic, the lesson strategy might move quickly from modeling directly to applying. The teacher asserts different roles according to the demands of the subject matter and the stage at which students are working.

A broad criticism of technology—perhaps especially app-driven tablet technology—is the extent to which it can be teacher-independent. There are also potential benefits to this, of course. But the image of parents using game or video apps to entertain their toddlers for a bit of quiet time conjures a comparable image of teachers using self-contained apps like the worksheets of old, simply to keep their students busy. "Independence" should not equate to "busywork."

Even with students functioning independently at the "You do, I watch" stage, there is a distinct difference between the teacher being a guide on the side and being wholly absent from the lesson activity. There is, after all, the "I watch" component, meaning that the teacher is monitoring independent learning, fine-tuning the lesson, and providing support as needed.

8.2 Phase 4: Implementation

Earlier in this book I suggested that the teacher—any learning designer—must not be merely a competent musician but a virtuoso. Virtuosos combine art and science, regardless of their field of endeavor. The virtuoso musician knows when to hold a note just a bit longer or push the vibrato beyond the written score. Knowing when to add a pinch of this spice or that herb, not mentioned in the recipe, distinguishes a chef from a cook.

Ross King (2000) recounts that when Arnolfo di Cambio designed the majestic Santa Maria del Fiore, the cathedral in Florence, Italy, in the thirteenth century, he had no idea how to construct the dome he envisioned to crown his magnificent building. He simply had faith that the technical knowledge would be developed when it was time to erect the dome. And so it was that more than a century later, along came Filippo Brunelleschi, a goldsmith with an interest in weights, wheels, and gears. At just the right moment in history, Brunelleschi combined artistry and technology, creating a gear system to raise the 108-ft high dome using some four million bricks. His achievement, now nearly six centuries later, still ranks as the largest brick dome in the world—truly a crowning achievement both for the cathedral and for Brunelleschi.

Learning designers sometimes are termed *learning architects*, and the term is fitting. Effective teachers design learning à la Brunelleschi, by combining art and science. Standards and curricula are blueprints, musical scores, and recipes—and virtuoso implementation requires the learning designer to apply nuances of artistic intuition along with technological science.

Helping students acquire simple knowledge may require little nuance, but the goals of truly effective teaching and learning aim higher on Bloom's taxonomy. Acquiring complex conceptual understanding requires students to accomplish the transition from "I do, you watch" to "You do, I watch" by participating in planning, monitoring, and fine-tuning their own learning processes. The implementation phase optimally should foster a learning partnership between teacher and student, in which the teacher provides support for each student's self-regulation of learning.

8.3 Fostering Students' Ownership of Learning

The notion that highly successful learners self-regulate their own learning ripples through the education literature. Self-regulated learning (SRL) is an iteration of constructivist theory and often can be thought of as students "owning" their own learning. SRL focuses on building self-awareness and learner autonomy over time (Paris & Paris, 2001). This process echoes the gradual release of responsibility model discussed previously.

The use of tablet technology adds a layer of complexity as well as opportunity. Tablets incorporate multimedia, directly involving visual, auditory, and kinesthetic processing. Students can see still and moving images on screen; hear sounds, music, and spoken language; and touch and manipulate onscreen objects using the touch-screen capability of the tablet. Consequently, multimedia requires students to integrate multisensory input (Ainsworth, Bibby, & Wood, 2002). Add the dimension of Internet connectivity and further navigation skills are required of the student (Cromley & Azevedo, 2009).

Australian researchers Ron Oliver and Jan Herrington (2003) summarize the point, saying, "Technology-based approaches to learning provide many opportunities for constructivist learning through their provision and support for resource-based, student-centered settings and by enabling learning to be related to context and to practice" (p. 12). Oliver and Herrington suggest a three-stage learning design process that involves (1) engaging tasks, (2) supports for learning, and (3) resources. The first and third of these have been dealt with in previous chapters. In considering supports, these researchers suggest that the teacher, as "coach and facilitator," develop supports in terms of scaffolding, which they define as a support system that "helps to build knowledge and is then removed as the knowledge construction occurs" (p. 14). The term *scaffold* neatly acknowledges the architectural aspect of learning design.

Scaffolding is, in essence, an iteration of the gradual release of responsibility model. The term *scaffolding* may be more familiar to readers, however. The following are some forms of scaffolding that teachers and students may find useful in implementing the learning design:

- *Suggesting a learning pathway.* This support could include suggesting strategies for dealing with resources, such as apps or website information.
- *Structuring opportunities for collaboration.* Working collaboratively in pairs or small groups may enable students to express their questions and reflect on new ideas in ways that increase both individual and collective learning.
- *Providing peer tutoring.* Particularly with younger students, peer tutoring can be a form of cooperative learning, with only nominal distance between tutor and tutee.
- *Using small-group and whole-class discussions.* These discussions provide times to share knowledge and understandings—and clear up misconceptions—at critical points during a lesson.

None of these supports presupposes a certain type of lesson or learning design, and they can be used with most types of subject matter and learners ranging from preschoolers to graduate students. Providing such supports helps students move through the construction of knowledge, from being watchers to becoming doers in the parlance of the gradual release of responsibility model.

## 8.4	Using Formative Feedback

Formative feedback involves the teacher functioning as a learning guide during a lesson in which students are working largely on their own. It is an element of scaffolding, an ongoing form of support. Formative feedback can be used to motivate, inform, or correct. The amount and intensity of feedback—high, low, or somewhere in between—will depend on the knowledge that students bring to the lesson (prior knowledge) and the conceptual complexity of the subject matter.

Spanish researchers Héctor García Rodicio, Emilio Sánchez, and Santiago R. Acuña (2013) conducted a small study involving undergraduate students that focused on the question: Do learners need extensive or minimal support for self-regulation in learning complex topics from multimedia explanations? This question is equally applicable to younger students and is appropriate in the context of this book because tablet technology epitomizes multimedia-mediated learning.

These researchers found that it was difficult for students to self-regulate learning when it came to complex topics conveyed through multimedia. "Learning complex conceptual systems with hypertext, multimedia, and hypermedia materials requires learners to deal with a number of difficulties," Rodicio and his colleagues wrote. The results of their experiment led them to conclude that "when low-prior-knowledge learners are expected to acquire complex conceptual systems, it seems critical to provide them with support for a broad spectrum of self-regulatory processes" (pp. 549–550). Experienced teachers probably recognize this conclusion intuitively, but the research is useful to point up the need to attend carefully to the role of technology in the implementation of the learning design.

The use of formative feedback during the implementation phase can be expressed in a basic matrix (see Fig. 8.1). If the subject matter has high conceptual complexity, students are more likely to need a higher level of formative feedback. They also will need higher formative feedback if they are approaching a topic about which they have little or no prior knowledge. If students have high prior knowledge or are working with subject matter that is relatively easy, or has low conceptual complexity, then they are likely to require only low formative feedback.

As Rodicio and his colleagues point out, the dimension of multimedia—for example, through the use of tablet technology—adds to conceptual complexity. Consequently, higher formative feedback may be needed initially, at least until tablet functions become second nature.

Let's suppose that students are working on the assignment that was posed as an example in Chap. 6: to locate, read, and summarize a nonfiction work by Mark Twain using a tablet computer. If students have not conducted an Internet search independently, then the first support might be to help them do just that. Prior knowledge of device functionality is low; therefore, high formative feedback may be needed to provide information, for instance, about trying various keywords and phrases. If a number of students are at a similar level of knowledge regarding tablet search functions, a scaffolding strategy might be to form a collaborative group so that students can share the formative feedback.

Fig. 8.1 Formative feedback
model

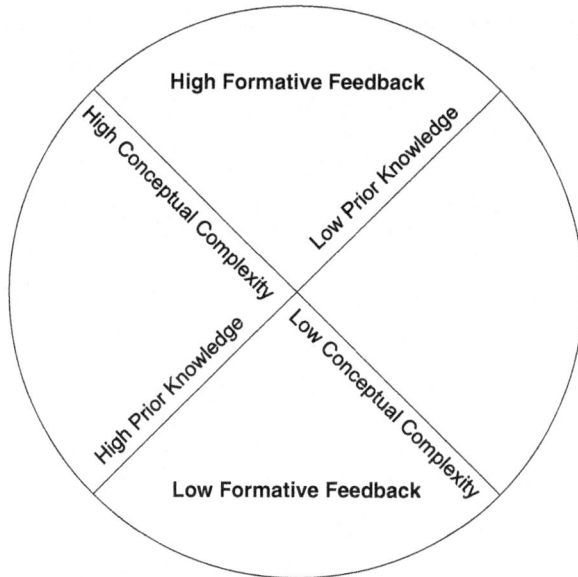

On the other hand, if Internet searching is an established skill (high prior knowledge), then formative feedback may revolve around conceptual complexity, for
instance, understanding how, first, to locate titles of Twain's nonfiction, then, to find
a full-text version, to skim the work and select a portion to summarize, and finally,
to compose the summary using a tablet app such as Pages (http://www.apple.com/
iwork/pages/), the iPad word-processing app. At any point during this procedure,
formative feedback may be necessary to help students successfully navigate the
complexity not only of the subject matter but of the multimedia used to access and
process information.

    If multimedia adds a layer of complexity, why use it? Consider that this research
endeavor would be complex even if done the "old-fashioned" way. Students would
need to locate and to navigate through encyclopedias, bibliographies, or other
research volumes; to find a physical copy of the target work; to skim it for a portion
to summarize; and to write the summary using pen and paper. Physical resources—
reference books, copies of Twain's writing—might be limited, and the process
would be time consuming—and only one or two students could be using the same
resource at the same time. Tablet technology allows each student to have access to
all of the resources, regardless whether other students are using them simultaneously. And using the tablet permits students to work at an individual pace best suited
to their abilities. Thus, while the assignment is complex in either case, the layer of
complexity added by using multimedia, once mastered, facilitates learning by offering enhanced access to more resources.

8.5   Summary

The implementation phase of the ADDIE model requires flexibility on the teacher's part in order for students to excel. The teacher/learning designer must be as observant during this phase as during the initial analysis phase. As the learning design unfolds, the teacher adopts various roles: model, guide, observer, and so on. The intent is to move students consistently from being watchers to becoming doers—independent, self-regulated learners. As architects of learning, teachers scaffold learning experiences to provide supports that help their students accomplish this transition in ways that involve the students both individually and collectively.

Observation informs timely intervention through the use of formative feedback. The extent of this feedback—whether low, high, or somewhere in between—will depend on students' prior knowledge and the conceptual complexity of the learning tasks. Both prior knowledge and conceptual complexity apply not only to subject matter and learning activities but also to the multimedia of tablet technology. While technology adds complexity, at least initially, it also facilitates learning by enhancing access to resources of all types.

References

Ainsworth, S., Bibby, P., & Wood, D. (2002). Examining the effects of different multiple representational systems in learning primary mathematics. *Journal of the Learning Sciences, 11*, 25–61.

Cromley, J. G., & Azevedo, R. (2009). Locating information within extended hypermedia. *Education Technology Research and Development, 57*, 287–313.

King, R. (2000). *Brunelleschi's dome: How a renaissance genius reinvented architecture*. New York: Penguin.

Oliver, R., & Herrington, J. (2003). Exploring technology-mediated learning from a pedagogical perspective. *Journal of Interactive Learning Environments, 11*, 111–126.

Paris, S., & Paris, A. (2001). Classroom applications of research on self-regulated learning. *Educational Psychologist, 36*(2001), 89–101.

Pearson, P. D., & Gallagher, M. C. (1983). The instruction of reading comprehension. *Contemporary Educational Psychology, 8*, 317–344.

Rodicio, H. G., Sánchez, E., & Acuña, S. R. (2013). Support for self-regulation in learning complex topics from multimedia explanations: Do learners need extensive or minimal support? *Instructional Science, 41*, 539–553.

Chapter 9
Evaluation: Before, During, and After

9.1 Introduction

Evaluation ensures that the learning design will accomplish, or has accomplished, the desired ends. The focus of the final *E—evaluation*—in the ADDIE model is on the learning design, not student achievement per se. Student achievement usually is an important element of design evaluation. But it is not the sole determinant of whether the learning design is successful.

In various formative and summative ways, evaluation is key to each step of the learning design process. In particular, the feedback loop of formative evaluation must be robust in order to maximize the match between the learners' needs and the intended goals of the lessons that compose the design. Chapter 6 introduced OPUS, an acronym for observe, probe, unify, and stage. These critical processes, as I mentioned in Chap. 8, are not for one-time use. They inform the entire ADDIE continuum, from analysis to evaluation. The formative information gleaned through these processes loops back to reshape the learning design as it unfolds.

When a learning design has been fully implemented and an end point has been reached, it is essential to allow time for active reflection. The term *active* is important, because it means that reflective summative evaluation should consist of more than sitting back and concluding, "That went well," or conversely, "That went badly." The arc of the gradual release of responsibility model—from "I do, you watch" to "You do, I watch"—often can frame the designer's reflection on the learning design. Summative evaluation ultimately not only determines the successes or failures of the specific learning design but also guides future iterations of that design and informs the creation of new designs.

9.2   Phase 5: Evaluation

Evaluation is a normal function of human existence. We look in a mirror and evaluate our appearance before we leave for work. We evaluate how well the vegetable garden is growing, whether the lawn needs mowing, and whether we should water or wait for rain. We evaluate our chances of crossing the street safely before we jaywalk. While we do not engage in a formal process, we evaluate *everything*.

Most of this evaluation is formative: reflect and respond. We don't like the way our tie looks with the jacket, so we change ties. We decide the radishes need to be thinned and the mower blade sharpened, but the rain prediction seems reliable enough that we won't bother watering. We consider the speed of the traffic and our aging knees and decide against jaywalking.

Why should it be different when it comes to learning design? The short answer is, it shouldn't. Formative evaluation should take place in each phase of the ADDIE model:

- Is the *analysis* accurate? Is it sufficient to guide the learning design?
- Is the *design* well matched to the analysis? Does it target the desired goals?
- Is the *development* consistent with the design goals? Does it incorporate appropriate resources and strategies that will foster student ownership of their learning?
- Is the *implementation* plan sufficient to match students' learning needs with lesson goals? Can adjustments be made or supports be provided to ensure maximum effectiveness as problems or issues arise?
- Is the *evaluation* consistent with the goals of the learning design? Does it provide sufficient information to guide future iterations of the same design as well as the creation of new designs for learning?

If the answer to any of these questions is negative, then the phase can be modified. Teachers ask students to use a similar reflect-and-respond strategy when they plan and carry out assignments and projects. One strategy is K-W-L: What do you *know*? What do you *want* to know? What did you *learn*? K-W-L was coined by Donna Ogle (1986) as a reading strategy, but it is widely applicable across the curriculum—and it ramps up to the learning design level as a way to guide teachers' active reflection.

In a very real sense, formative evaluation is the comprehensive, self-reflective counterpart to formative feedback, which was detailed in Chap. 12. Formative feedback involved the teacher/learning designer observing students' activities during the implementation phase and providing supports to modify implementation. Formative evaluation incorporates opportunities throughout the ADDIE sequence for the designer to evaluate—that is, to reflect on what has happened, is happening, or is likely to happen—and to respond accordingly. The response may be to do nothing because the design is unfolding as conceived and everything is A-OK. Or the response may be a course correction—a new support, a different approach, an alternative resource, and so on.

The questions above are illustrative. Potential evaluative questions vary over a considerable range, depending on the actual learning design. Let's go back to the lesson idea in Chap 6: to locate, read, and summarize a nonfiction work by Mark Twain using a tablet computer. In Chap. 8, when this example was used during the implementation phase, I suggested several possible points of entry for this lesson. One might be to help students learn how to do an effective Internet search if they have had little experience with that function. Formative feedback might indicate a need for one or two learning supports, for instance, the teacher modeling an Internet search or structuring a small-group brainstorming session to generate potential keywords.

Formative evaluation requires the teacher to reflect on whether this portion of the implementation phase worked: Were some students Internet-savvy and others not? If so, how was instruction differentiated? Once the teacher modeled Internet searching, were students able to search independently? Will additional modeling or guided practice be needed in the future? If so, could some students who have mastered Internet searching mentor other students who need additional modeling and practice?

Within a tablet environment—or any technology-mediated learning situation—formative evaluation must consider students' development of technology skills alongside content knowledge acquisition.

9.3 The Test as Summative Evaluation

Formative evaluation is used to shape, or reshape, the learning design as it unfolds. But what about summative evaluation? Isn't a test sufficient to judge whether the goals of a learning design have been reached?

Student achievement is an important indicator in the overall evaluation of a learning design. It is not the only indicator. And a test is not the only way to evaluate student achievement. Indeed, a poorly designed test can be a faulty way to evaluate both student learning and the learning design. Tests can be simple and easy to use, but just as often, they are simplistic and simply wrong.

Over the past two decades, a burgeoning testing industry has fostered a culture in which The Test—often a standardized test—is the sole or primary vehicle for evaluation. Many politicians and pundits, mostly non-educators, along with a surprising number of educators have gravitated toward this simplistic strategy that often misjudges students' accomplishments and is misused to judge other educational factors, including teacher competence and school or district success.

Harris, Smith, and Harris (2011) point out that "the inherent unfairness of allowing the scores on standardized tests to be our primary—in some cases, our only—way of judging school quality is one of the cruel ironies of the way public education in America has evolved" (p. 45). They are not alone in taking this view. Using tests to judge teacher effectiveness, for example, "assumes that student learning is measured well by a given test, is influenced by the teacher alone, and is independent from the growth of classmates and other aspects of the classroom context" (Darling-Hammond, Amrein-Beardsley, Haertel, & Rothstein, 2012, p. 8). The same could be said of using a test to determine the effectiveness of a learning design. It's simply too limiting, and the information derived through a test alone can be misleading. The alternative is a multifaceted evaluation.

9.4 Multifaceted Summative Evaluation

Clearly, the learning designer who wants to understand and fully evaluate a learning design must adopt a multifaceted approach. I would pose this challenge in terms of a new Three R's: reactions, responses, and results. These Three R's can be characterized as follows:

- What *reactions* did students have to the learning design? Did they like the learning process? Were they engaged? Were they motivated to go beyond the basic requirements of the lessons?
- What *responses* resulted from the learning design? How did students go about learning? What behaviors did they engage in? Were students able to learn independently? Cooperatively?
- What *results* were achieved by the learning design? What did students learn? Were the goals of the learning design accomplished? Can future learning designs build on this one?

The following are several ways to answer these types of evaluative questions:

Observations. Just as in the OPUS strategy, observing students can provide many indications of whether a learning design has been effective. While observation early on can lead to changes, such as adding supports, in summative evaluation, it is focused on the total arc of the design. Did students move from questioning or hesitant to capable and confident? Do they evidence a sense of accomplishment, a desire to move forward and learn more; or conversely, are they frustrated or confused, discouraged or bored? In either case, teachers can draw conclusions about the effectiveness of the learning design and glean information to help shape future designs.

Discussions. One-on-one, small-group, and whole-class debriefing sessions allow students opportunities to talk about their lesson experiences. What were the pluses and the minuses? Teachers who use active listening and probe for salient details can gather a wealth of information from such discussions. Moreover, these summative discussions also allow students to listen to one another, which has the potential for further enriching the learning experience. For example, if students have worked in small groups, one member might report on a learning strategy that their group used. Other groups, hearing about the experience, may respond with, "We didn't think of that, but here's what we did…." Discussions transform the summative evaluation from an instance of information gathering by the teacher into a shared learning experience for the teacher and the students.

Reflective Questions. K-W-L-type questions, mentioned previously, provide an effective basis for reflection by students on their learning experiences, which in turn can help the teacher evaluate the learning design, as well as to evaluate students' learning. The teacher might take the general knowledge question, for example, and make it specific: "What did you know about doing an Internet search before we started this lesson?" "What did you want to know about using the Internet to find information?" And, "What did you learn about Internet searching?" In positioning tablet technology as a toolbox for learning, these questions about students' comfort and competence with technological functions—using the Internet, using specific apps—are as important as questions about content knowledge and skills acquisition. Of course, the same strategy applies to content: "What did you know about Mark Twain's nonfiction before this unit of study?" "What did you want to learn about Mark Twain's work?" "What did you learn about Twain's nonfiction writings?"

Tests. While complex learning often can be better understood using observations, discussions, and reflective questions, teacher-made tests can be effective for examining students' basic knowledge of both content and technology. A summative test might ask questions such as the following: What is a keyword? How are fiction and nonfiction different? Technology tools can help. For example, teachers with Google accounts can create tests using Google Forms (http://www.google.com/drive/apps. html). Forms provide a template that facilitates creating tests with multiple-choice, text, and other types of responses. It also will aggregate responses in several ways. The program works on tablets and other computers.

Questionnaires. Students also can be asked to reflect on their learning experience by responding to a questionnaire. Reflective questions, as suggested above, can be answered verbally or in writing. The answers in either case tend to be discursive. Questionnaires may be more focused than open discussions but also can run the risk of providing few details. The contrast might be compared to the difference between a still photo and a video. Nonetheless, questionnaires can be productive, are usually easy for the teacher to construct, and the recorded responses that can be considered over time. A questionnaire might focus on learning strategies, involvement or engagement, affect (how students feel about the lessons), materials, or other aspects of the learning design. For instance, the teacher might use a combination of discussion and testing to evaluate whether the design achieved content-acquisition goals but use reflective questions and a questionnaire to better understand students' facility with and feelings about the technology they used. Google Forms, mentioned above, can facilitate questionnaire design, as can other programs, such as Survey Monkey (http://www.surveymonkey.com).

9.5 Summary

Robust formative and summative evaluation ensures that the learning design is accomplishing (during its unfolding) and has accomplished (at its conclusion) the intended goals. Student achievement is an important element of design evaluation, but it is not the sole determinant of whether a learning design is successful. Sometimes content knowledge acquisition is a secondary goal. It would be narrow and simplistic to think of learning only in terms of knowing more "stuff." Content acquisition is enhanced when teachers/learning designers and others involved in the educative process attend to integral factors, such as affect (liking the subject, the device), environment (comfortable surroundings, adequate resources), ethos (how teachers and students interact with one another), and processes (learning strategies, technological functions). Examining all of these factors is the full intent of the final E in the ADDIE model.

References

Darling-Hammond, L., Amrein-Beardsley, A., Haertel, E., & Rothstein, J. (2012). Evaluating teacher evaluation. *Phi Delta Kappan, 93*, 8–15.

Harris, P., Smith, B. M., & Harris, J. (2011). *The myths of standardized tests: Why they don't tell you what you think they do*. New York: Rowman and Littlefield.

Ogle, D. M. (1986). K-W-L: A teaching model that develops active reading of expository text. *Reading Teacher, 39*, 564–570.

Chapter 10
Are eTextbooks More Than Books?

10.1   Introduction

The question posed in the title of this chapter can be answered "yes" in several ways. Electronic textbooks, or eTextbooks, like their more general e-book counterparts, vary enormously along a continuum of interactivity. Imagine this: If you can take an empty picture frame, lay the glass over a textbook page, and have almost exactly what you see using an e-reader, then that is what you get with basic digitized text. On one hand, there is still value in such an eTextbook. But the value is related to cost and availability, not interactivity. This is the position at one end of the interactivity continuum. It is the same position occupied by most general-purpose e-books. They offer lower cost and greater portability but little else in comparison to standard paperback and hardcover books.

The best eTextbooks, on the other hand, incorporate interactivity and multisensory components that cannot be found in traditional print textbooks. These features also confirm the teaching and learning advantages of using tablet computers. Tablets, such as Apple's iPad, incorporate e-reader functionality using multiple platforms, such as Kindle, Nook, and others, but also do much more because they are fully operational computers. As such, tablets facilitate high-end eTextbook functionality, such as linking text directly to the Internet and allowing note-sharing across devices.

This chapter explores a range of ways that e-books and eTextbooks can ramp up teaching and learning for tablet classrooms. These digital resources offer many opportunities—and challenges—for learning designers at all levels of education.

10.2   A Digital Starting Point

Let's begin at the low-interactivity end of the e-book continuum. The previous illustration—laying an empty picture frame over a printed page and seeing essentially the same thing on an e-reader—fairly accurately represents the starting point

D.R. Walling, *Designing Learning for Tablet Classrooms: Innovations in Instruction*,   55
DOI 10.1007/978-3-319-02420-2_10, © Springer International Publishing Switzerland 2014

of the continuum of digital interactivity. The value of low-tech digitized texts is related to cost and availability, not to interactivity. But these factors alone point to e-books being more than "books," meaning traditional print publications.

For example, if a teacher's "textbooks" actually are individual chapters or articles or commercial books, such as historical essays in a civic education class or novels in an English class, then the low cost and ready availability of e-books offer a distinct advantage over having students buy print books or try to find a sufficient quantity (such as a class set) in the school library. Consider a lesson in which the students are to read and discuss a classic novel, such as Jane Austen's *Pride and Prejudice*. This book is widely available in relatively inexpensive paperback editions from a variety of publishers because it is long out of copyright. A quick search for this title on the popular Amazon.com bookselling website will yield a range of available volumes—various editions and bindings—both new and used. On the day I checked, a typical new paperback edition of Austen's novel cost $8.99, with an e-book edition, delivered through Kindle, running only $2.56.

However, because this novel is a classic long out of copyright, it also is available through several online, free digital providers. One example is Project Gutenberg (http://www.gutenberg.org), from which *Pride and Prejudice* can be downloaded in a myriad of formats: HTML, EPUB, Kindle, PDF, Plucker, QiOO Mobile, plain text, and so on. The book also can simply be read online through the Gutenberg website. All of these options are at no cost. The downloads are virtually instantaneous. And it does not matter whether the class includes 3 students or 30; they can all be reading the same novel at the same time. Best of all, Project Gutenberg offers more than 42,000 free e-books in several hundred categories and in Portuguese and German as well as English.

The low cost (often free) and availability of such basic resources are a boon to cash-strapped schools, but of course there are limits. Free digital books tend to be older works, such as classic novels and historical documents. Learning designers and teachers whose students need access to recent texts and up-to-the-minute information will need to move further along the interactivity continuum.

10.3   Enhanced eTextbooks

Higher education has taken the lead in moving toward electronic textbooks. In 2011, for example, the interactive textbook app Inkling (https://www.inkling.com) announced partnerships with McGraw-Hill and Pearson Education, two of the major players in the higher education textbook market. Both publishers were set to move forward on producing "enhanced" eTextbooks. "Enhanced" refers to digitized textbooks that incorporate various degrees of interactivity. According to *Digital Book World*'s Yvette Chin (2011), features that set Inkling's efforts apart "are their 'natively digital' origins and built-in interactivity features." Chin writes, "Rather than being a more or less faithful electronic version of a traditional print textbook, Inkling incorporates multimedia elements, including video and 3D objects, to enhance the learning experience."

In 2012, Apple announced a similar move, developing partnerships with three major US textbook publishers to develop interactive textbooks for the K-12 school market. More such partnerships—at all levels—are likely over time. Whether for first-graders or college co-eds, the movers in the interactive textbook world are convinced that such resources complement how today's Digital Age students learn. For example, an interactive eTextbook about music appreciation will incorporate integrated soundtracks by classical composers. Science students can use tablet computer functionality to zoom in on detailed 3D images of everything from insect larvae in their nests to organs in the human body.

Interactivity enhances students' acquisition of knowledge and understanding by tapping multiple senses. Enhanced digital textbooks move beyond merely reading for information. Students can study still and moving images; listen to sounds, spoken words, and music; use touch to manipulate onscreen elements; add notes directly to textbook content; connect to the Internet to search out related information; and share ideas and content with their teachers and classmates. In addition to direct learning-related advantages of eTextbooks over traditional print, there are collateral benefits:

Lower costs. Electronic textbooks usually are less expensive, often much less, than their print counterparts. Adding interactive elements to traditional textbook programs, such as supplementary videos, often has meant adding costs as well. And such elements usually are designed for group use, rather than individual use. eTextbooks that are fully interactive do not require the purchase of expensive supplementary elements because multimedia are built in. And the media can be accessed by individual student users.

Updated content. The high price of traditional print textbooks forces schools to use textbooks for several years. In recent times, schools hard-pressed by budget constraints often have pushed beyond 3- to 5-year adoption cycles to 6- to 8-year cycles or longer, meaning that textbooks often are obsolete during the later years of the cycle. By contrast, downloading updated content can be virtually instantaneous (similar to the way app updates are delivered to iPads and other tablet devices) and many times can be accomplished at little or no additional cost.

Lighter loads. Students, parents, teachers, and health authorities have long complained about the increasing weight that students are expected to carry in school satchels and backpacks. Textbooks are heavy, and many students routinely carry several at a time. This is not only a US problem. A 2012 study of children in Spain, for example, found that a majority of children carried backpacks exceeding 10 % of their body weight, and those carrying the heaviest backpacks had a 50 % higher risk of back pain. They also had an increased risk of back pathology, or long-term back problems (Rodríguez-Oviedo et al. 2012). When all or most of a student's required textbooks can be carried electronically on a single tablet computer, the weight of a typical backpack can easily be reduced from 30 or 40 pounds to 2 or 3 pounds.

In February 2012, the chairman of the Federal Communications Commission (FCC) and the US Secretary of Education unveiled a *Digital Textbook Playbook* (http://www.fcc.gov/encyclopedia/digital-textbook-playbook), designed to help

US schools make the transition to digital textbooks. The *Playbook* provides guidelines, background information, and resources that schools can use to move away from the burdens associated with print textbooks to achieve the benefits of Digital Age eTextbooks.

10.4   Customizing eTextbooks

The authors of the *NMC Horizon Report* comment, "Student-specific data can now be used to customize curricula and suggest resources to students in the same way that businesses tailor advertisements and offers to customers" (Johnson et al., 2013, p. 4). This principle extends to learning designers' ability to customize students' textbooks by thinking outside the "book." Interactivity already places eTextbooks outside the standard confines of print. The next logical step along the interactivity continuum is to allow schools, districts, and individual teachers to adapt existing textbooks and to create customized textbooks using digital technology.

Many teachers already adapt textbooks in some manner, for instance, by using only certain chapters or reordering chapters to better suit a sequence of instruction. For certain lessons, teachers also may provide supplementary materials, such as suggested readings, organizational charts, or illustrations. This form of adaptation can be accomplished as easily—indeed, often more easily—through digital technology. For example, teachers and students can use cloud-based storage and sharing applications, where teachers can upload supplemental materials that can be accessed by students whether they are in the classroom, at home, or elsewhere. One such free application is Dropbox (http://www.dropbox.com), which recently expanded service to educators with .edu e-mail addresses to allow extra storage space.

The interactivity of Dropbox provides not only for teachers to convey information to students but also the other way around. Students can use the app as a way to turn in homework or share files with other students. The widespread use of Dropbox has led to integration ("syncing") with other apps, such as Evernote (http://evernote.com), a well-regarded note-taking/note-sharing program.

Google Apps for Education (http://www.google.com/enterprise/apps/education/) offers a suite of teacher- and student-friendly apps, including Google Drive, which functions similar to Dropbox. Both Dropbox and Google Drive are available for a range of tablet devices.

10.5   Creating eTextbooks

While the major textbook publishers now produce electronic versions of their textbooks, many experts believe that the future lies in another direction. Some publishers, incidentally, are inadvertently propelling this option by requiring schools to purchase standard print books in order to gain access to digital content. "The long-term transformation is not books going online," according to Mary Skafidas, a marketing executive at McGraw-Hill. She continues, "It's the creation of different tools, a step beyond digital prose. We have gone beyond that to create simulations, math disguised as video games, and whole digital worlds" (Rix, 2011). Textbook publishers, in fact, may be left behind as the open education movement continues to grow and as schools and even states move away from traditional textbook adoption.

Today, more and more learning designers are creating their own eTextbooks, often in collaboration with students and other teachers, by gathering the electronic resources and courseware they need to address particular curricula. Resources include articles found online, simulations, and audio and video files. These may be supplemented by lesson plans shared by other educators. Although building an eTextbook in this manner can be labor intensive and time consuming, the result can be a uniquely suitable, targeted, and well-tailored learning resource.

An eTextbook can be structured like a traditional book using e-book publishing strategies. A variety of programs exist that can facilitate the creation of an e-book that can be used across multiple platforms. One example is ePub Bud (http://www.epub-bud.com), which also features e-books for free download, including a number of children's books. Amazon's Kindle Direct Publishing (http://kdp.amazon.com) can be used to create e-books for Kindle devices or apps, and Barnes and Noble's Nook Press (formerly PubIt, http://www.nookpress.com) can be used similarly to create e-books for Nook devices and apps. Finally, iBooks Author (http://www.apple.com/ibooks-author/) facilitates multi-touch eTextbooks for the iPad and other Apple devices.

Alternatively, an eTextbook need not look like a traditional book at all. Learning designers and teachers at all levels can become digital curators, rather than publishers per se, by gathering sources of information into collections that more closely resemble digital libraries than individual books. LiveBinders (http://www.livebinders.com), for example, helps users collect and organize resources, from article files to demonstrations and simulations. Wiki tools can accomplish similar ends—collecting and organizing a resource repository—and include Google Sites (http://sites.google.com), PBworks (http://pbworks.com), and Wikispaces (http://www.wikispaces.com).

Learning designers who want to combine existing education apps, including entire courses of study, with customized content may find that Apple's iTunes U (http://www.apple.com/education/itunes-u/) is a good fit, whether students are first graders, graduate students, or somewhere in between. iTunes U is a powerful app for building courses. Within the app, students can read books and articles, listen to audio of readings or lectures, view videos, take notes, and work through a checklist of assignments. Teachers can send messages to students and post assignments, and students receive a notification. Onscreen instructions walk learning designers through the process of creating and delivering a course that subsequently can be modified and updated whenever necessary. Consequently, while the up-front effort may be considerable, over the long term, a "book" or "library" created in this manner should have extended usability.

The transformation of textbooks continues to spawn new ways to deliver content and new providers who can help. For example, CK-12 (http://www.ck12.org) is a nonprofit organization founded in 2008 that offers open content in STEM (science, technology, engineering, mathematics) subjects, configured as "FlexBooks." The organization's FlexBook System provides an online platform for creating interactive eTextbooks.

In addition to all of the advantages already mentioned, customized eTextbooks also permit learning designers to align content with local, state, or national learning standards and curricula and, concurrently, to match content and learning strategies to the identified needs and interests of students.

10.6   Summary

Are eTextbooks more than books? Absolutely. Electronic textbooks may resemble print books with pages of text that actually flip in the more sophisticated programs. But there the resemblance ends. Even at the low end of the interactivity continuum, many e-book programs provide for text highlighting, instant access to dictionary definitions, video and audio instead of still photos, and links to online content that expands on ideas in the text. Students with vision issues can benefit from e-reader features that allow the user to enlarge the size of the text and alter background and letter tones. And all students can avoid a lifetime of back pain associated with carrying backpacks full of heavy traditional textbooks.

Earlier in this book, I suggested that iPads and other types of tablet computers should be viewed not merely as tools but, more accurately, as toolboxes full of many and varied technological tools. Analogous to this idea is that eTextbooks are not merely digital versions of print textbooks. On the contrary, they are digital libraries stocked with many different types of resources. Learning designers, teachers, and even students must become curators as well as users to benefit fully from this abundance of resources for teaching and learning.

References

Chin, Y. (2011, March 31). An inkling of the future? Enhanced ebooks and the college textbook market. *Digital Book World (dbw)*. Retrieved October 24, 2013, from http://www.digitalbookworld.com/2011/an-inkling-of-the-future-enhanced-ebooks-and-the-college-textbook-market/

Digital Textbook Collaborative. (2012, February 1). *Digital Textbook Playbook*. Retrieved October 24, 2013, from http://transition.fcc.gov/files/Digital_Textbook_Playbook.pdf

Johnson, L., Adams Becker, S., Cummins, M., Estrada, V., Freeman, A., & Ludgate, H. (2013). *NMC Horizon Report: 2013 K-12 Edition*. Austin, Texas: New Media Consortium.

Rix, K. (2011, Winter) Build Your Own Digital Textbooks. *Scholastic Administr@tor Magazine*. http://www.scholastic.com

Rodríguez-Oviedo, P., Ruano-Ravina, A., Pérez-Rios, M., Garcia, F.B., Gómez-Fernández, D., Fernández-Alonzo, A., et al. (2012, August). School children's backpacks, back pain and back pathologies. *Archives of Disease in Childhood, 97*, 730–732.

Chapter 11
Tablet Computer Reading: The How's

11.1 Introduction

Tablet computers are changing how teachers conduct reading instruction in every sense. Tablets are being used at school—and at home in many instances—to teach reading basics, both primary and remedial, and to extend and enhance reading skills while students read for knowledge and understanding as they move through the grades. Tablets also are being used as assistive technology for students with disabilities, such as mobility issues. While an in-depth discussion of reading instruction is beyond the scope of this book, it is important to consider how tablet technology can assist all readers but especially those in the beginning stages and those who may be struggling with reading skills or with particular subject matter. The how's are the topic of this chapter. In Chap. 12, I will take up the what's—what there is to read on a tablet computer.

In the previous chapter, the focus was on eTextbooks and how the very concept of textbooks—how they are created and who creates them—is changing to complement Digital Age learning. Textbooks of any kind, of course, are only a portion of the reading materials that initially constitute learning to read and thereafter are read to learn—and not incidentally to polish reading skills throughout the grades and into higher education.

As interactivity and multimedia are woven into texts, reading words on a screen is becoming a distinctly different experience compared to reading words on a page. Some observers express concerns that the act of reading—thus the development of reading skills and an appreciation for reading—is being forced into the backseat, and what really drives many early reading apps and e-books on tablet computers is multimedia, not text. In considering the how's of tablet computer reading, it is necessary to give these concerns appropriate attention.

D.R. Walling, *Designing Learning for Tablet Classrooms: Innovations in Instruction*,   61
DOI 10.1007/978-3-319-02420-2_11, © Springer International Publishing Switzerland 2014

11.2   Early Reading

Teachers and parents expressed concerns about how young children learn to read in the Digital Age even before tablet computers made e-books for early reading development more accessible than through other devices. Tablets have encouraged and facilitated e-books for all ages and levels of reading development, and so teachers' and parents' concerns have increased accordingly—and they are not without merit. In general, the concerns revolve around whether learning to read is helped or hindered by e-books, and the question often comes down to whether e-books are really about reading.

Lisa Guernsey, director of the Early Education Initiative at the New America Foundation, took up this question in a *School Library Journal* article and reviewed a number of perspectives. She noted a couple of questions that teachers, parents, librarians, reading specialists, and learning designers of all sorts need to bear in mind when considering tablet-based e-books for reading instruction or remediation—namely, "Which, if any, [interactive] features are necessary to enhance engagement and improve a child's comprehension of the story? Which ones are nothing more than distractions, eye candy, elements that derail the very act of reading?" (Guernsey, 2011).

Those are critical questions. For example, an e-book that is one-quarter text and three-quarters media (audio and video clips or animation) may captivate young learners, but do children who interact with such e-books actually engage with the text? Or are they merely being entertained by the multimedia components? Because e-books are still relatively new, this is a concern that has not been answered by comprehensive research. This concern, however, follows on a more basic question: What is an e-book?

There is no such thing as a "standard" e-book. As I noted in the previous chapter on eTextbooks, digital books of all varieties run the gamut from straightforward digitized text, such as PDF versions of print books, to fully interactive, multimedia e-books (or full-fledged apps) in which audiovisual components and touchscreen manipulation of objects and animations dominate a minimal amount of text. If the goal is to teach conceptual knowledge and understandings, then the more "bells and whistles" in terms of multimedia, the better, because multimedia engage multiple senses and tap more modes of learning. This is a point that I have emphasized elsewhere in the context of writing instruction, but it applies equally to reading instruction (see Walling, 2006). Effective learning design must be multimodal to be optimally effective with all students, not just those students whose best mode of learning is visual and text oriented.

By contrast, if the focus is to help students fully engage with text itself, whether words on a page or words on a screen, then it makes sense to be selective regarding the kind and amount of multimedia to incorporate. Too much non-text content may be counterproductive.

The decision chart in Fig. 11.1 is intended to assist learning designers in considering the type of book format that is likely to be most effective. Included are

Book Format Decision Chart

Target Learner(s): _____

Learning Component	Print Book with Text Only	Print Book with Visual Cues	eBook with Audio Cues or Links	eBook with Visual Cues or Links	eBook with Dictionary Links	eBook with Web Links
Phonemic awareness						
Phonics						
Fluency						
Vocabulary						
Comprehension						

Fig. 11.1 Book format decision chart

categories for print books with text only, print books with visual cues (such as illustration and photos), e-books with audio cues or links (such as embedded sound clips or links to such clips on the Internet), e-books with visual cues (photos, illustrations, or links to such visuals online), e-books with dictionary links (often built in to e-reader software apps), and e-books with Web links (for additional resources, more in-depth content, and so forth).

The five learning components listed in this Book Format Decision Chart—phonemic awareness, phonics, fluency, vocabulary, and comprehension—are based on generally accepted research on reading instruction (Learning Point Associates, 2004; see also AFT, 1999). This chart is specific to reading for purposes of this chapter, but it could readily be adapted for other subject matter and the learning components specific to that subject. For instance, what learning components are specific to mathematics, and what book format(s) would be most helpful for each of those components? The components might also be adapted to incorporate more specific local, state, or national standards.

To use the decision chart effectively, it is essential to identify the target learner(s), an individual or a pair or group of learners with similar learning needs and characteristics. Likewise, from the learning designer's perspective, it also is essential to identify how the teacher plans to go about the task of instruction. These two characteristics will influence decisions in each of the component categories.

Let's consider an example. The teacher identifies a group of three or four students who are having similar difficulty with basic alphabetics—phonemic awareness, let's say. In designing learning for this group, the teacher decides to begin with direct instruction: just the teacher and the book. So the first book format decision may be to use a print book with text only. In the chart, the learning designer could enter "1" in the column "Print Book with Text Only." Later on, because the teacher wants the students to practice on their own and recognizes that such practice might be most effective with audio support, an e-book with audio cues that the student can activate to recall sound-letter correspondence would be more effective than a print book that has only text. Consequently, the learning designer would enter "2" in the column "eBook with Audio Cues or Links." This two-step decision may be all that the learning designer wants to complete prior to formative assessment to determine how to move forward.

This type of decision-making is an aspect of digital curation. A curator selects and cares for a selection of materials. The word *curator* comes from Latin *curare*, "take care." Today's librarians increasingly are expected to be digital curators as school, university, and public libraries expand their collections to include e-books and other digital materials. But curation responsibilities are not restricted to librarians. Learning designers of every stripe also must be curators of the resources that they will use to develop their designs for learning.

The learning designer's individual planning strategy should dictate whether to complete the whole decision chart in one go or in stages, perhaps as lessons unfold over the course of time. And, of course, some decisions regarding book format also will depend on available resources. While an e-book with audio cues might be ideal for independent student practice with phonemic awareness, there is no guarantee that such a book will be available or, if available, affordable. The range of available e-books is expanding exponentially, but it still has limits.

11.3 Remedial and Special-Purpose Reading

Tablet technology, simply by moving the computer from atop a desk directly into the students' hands, makes interactions both with the technology itself and with digital content more personal and individual. This individualization crosses even traditional small-group practices, such as shared reading. A small study of shared reading with preschoolers using iPads instead of print books found the transition to new media easy (although teachers occasionally needed to help students stay focused on text because of the device's other attractions). The researchers concluded, among other things, that "ebook pedagogy will likely be a hybrid of old and new reading instruction practices" (Roskos & Burstein, 2012, p. 49). This notion of hybrid teaching and learning is an important holistic understanding of the use of tablet technology.

Throughout this book, my intent is to examine learning design for incorporating tablet technology into real schools, not imaginary, somewhere-in-the-future schools. Proven strategies for teaching and learning can be enhanced—sometime even transformed—by using tablet technology. But tablet classrooms are not some mythical future of education; they are the present in many schools today and the very near future in many more.

For students who require remedial instruction in reading, their difficulties may be rooted in difficulty learning through traditional, non-tablet means. Consequently, the simple introduction of a new device may stimulate new learning through higher motivation, more support for multisensory input, and increased independent practice. Multisensory, manipulative letter and word experiences, in particular, often hold the key to assisting students who are experiencing initial reading delays.

A growing number of tablet apps can supply both teacher-led and independent learning assistance with basic reading skills and strategies. A sample approach can be illustrated with an app called Word Wagon (http://www.duckduckmoose.com/educational-iphone-itouch-apps-for-kids/word-wagon/) from Duck Duck Moose, a company that creates child-centered education apps for Apple and Android devices. According to the product description, Word Wagon, for ages one to seven, "includes 103 words (including 44 Dolch sight words)" in seven categories, such as colors and numbers. The app is organized in four levels: letters, phonics, spelling 1, and spelling 2. The story framework of the app involves Mozzarella the mouse and his best friend Coco the bird, who play with letters, words, and phonics. The animated characters' playtime resembles typical play among young children: playing hide and seek, dressing up, talking on the phone, and so on.

For busy teachers, education apps like Word Wagon that students can use independently are extraordinarily helpful in individualizing instruction, which is especially important to meet the needs of struggling readers.

The same multimedia features that make such apps good for struggling readers also make them a good fit for students with special needs. Students with limited range of physical motion, for example, often can easily manipulate the one-finger touch or swipe necessary to activate touchscreen applications. Additionally, there are specialized apps designed to assist teachers in working with students who have specific disabilities.

Consider nonverbal learning disability (NVLD or NLD), which often presents as difficulties with motor skills, visual perception, and spatial organization. Such difficulties interfere with learning to read. A number of apps are available to assist, including one called abc PocketPhonics (http://www.appsinmypocket.com/pocketphonics/index.html), from appsinmypocket.com. The app teaches letter sounds, and students write letters and blend letter sounds to form words. Interestingly, the app features cursive letters that the student user traces with one finger. The use of cursive, rather than print, is helpful for students with fine motor difficulties because of the smoother flow of the curving letters.

As the number and variety of tablet apps grows, it is becoming increasingly easier for learning designers to find just the right approach that can improve learning for students with particular needs that may not be met by conventional instruction. There is a further discussion of multisensory learning in Chap. 15.

11.4 Enhanced Comprehension

For students of all ages, reading comprehension can be improved in most cases by attaching a visual to a concept. It is a way to make the abstract more concrete and thus easier to understand and remember. Consequently, a popular comprehension-building strategy is mental mapping, or mind mapping. This is a useful example of how tablet technology can be used to build reading strategies well beyond the basics of learning to read.

Mind maps are essentially visually organizers. (Use the keyword "mind mapping" to find sample images online.) Many mind-mapping apps are available, such as MindMeister (http://www.mindmeister.com/mobile), which works with Apple and Android devices. This tablet app allows the user to create, view, and edit maps; organize them into folders; and share them with others.

Another possibility, especially for teachers who want students working on desktop or laptop computers to be able to use a variety of mind-mapping programs, is to use an app for the teacher's tablet that allows imports from several different programs. For example, iThoughtsHD (http://www.ithoughts.co.uk/iThoughtsHD/Welcome.html) is specifically designed for the iPad and, according to the website, "will import and export mindmaps to and from many of the most popular desktop mindmap applications such as MyThoughts, Freemind, Freeplane, XMind, Novamind, MindManager, MindView, ConceptDraw MINDMAP, MindGenius and iMindmap." This type of app can help in situations where schools or classrooms are transitioning from desktop or laptop computers to 1:1 tablets for students.

Learning designers have dozens of choices of free and paid apps for various devices that help students use mind mapping to increase knowledge and understanding— not only as an essential reading strategy in the early grades but also as a continuing learning strategy throughout their education.

Some apps are better for younger students, some for more mature learners. While sorting through this maze can be time-consuming and tedious, it also offers the learning designer the opportunity to find apps that are not just almost right but exactly right for individual learners and specific learning contexts. One helpful note: App producers' websites often feature introductory videos, as do the MindMeister and iThoughtsHD websites mentioned above, which review the main features of the app, thus allowing the learning designer to determine fairly quickly whether the app is right for the intended purpose.

11.5 Summary

The nature of tablet technology offers learning designers many options for working with reading skills and strategies across various populations of learners and the full range of subject matter. From the youngest to the most mature learners, students regardless of ability or disability can be matched to learning materials that meet their needs and interests as tablet technology continues to develop. This is not hyperbole; however, it should be remembered that tablet computers are still very new. While the number and variety of apps and e-books is growing exponentially, gaps still exist.

At the same time, creative learning designers may be able to repurpose apps and e-books to use in contexts beyond those for which they were conceived. Figure 11.1 offers a way to structure both critical and creative thinking about book decisions. This framework can be adapted for thinking about how to design learning in other contexts as well.

Interactivity and multimedia are key components of tablet functionality. But, in the context of reading, it also is important for learning designers to consider when these components may get in the way of learning. As in any field of endeavor, the more choices that are available, the more crucial it is to think carefully about matching technology and techniques—the how's—to learning objectives.

References

American Federation of Teachers (AFT). (1999). *Teaching reading is rocket science: What expert teachers of reading should know and be able to do*. Washington, DC: Author http://www.aft.org

Guernsey, L. (2011, June 7). Are ebooks any good? *School Library Journal*. Retrieved July 1, 2013 from http://www.slj.com/2011/06/ebooks/are-ebooks-any-good/

Learning Point Associates. (2004). *A closer look at the five essential components of effective reading instruction: A review of scientifically based reading research for teachers*. Naperville, IL: Author, http://www.learningpt.org

Roskos, K., & Burstein, K. (2012) Descriptive observations of ebook shared reading at preschool. *Journal of Literacy and Technology 13* 27–57. http://www.literacyandtechnology.org

Walling, D. R. (2006). *Teaching writing to visual, auditory, and kinesthetic learners*. Thousand Oaks, CA: Corwin.

Chapter 12
Tablet Computer Reading: The What's

12.1 Introduction

The previous chapters have focused on e-books and eTextbooks, concentrating on the how's of tablet computer reading: how the act of reading, or learning to read, is altered in the transition from print to digital and how the reading matter is presented in a tablet environment. Peripherally, I have included a few suggestions regarding what is available to read. In this chapter, the what's are the focus. The central question is, what kinds of reading matter are available across the curriculum?

In Chap. 11, I suggested that the nature of tablet technology provides learning designers with many options for using reading as a doorway into acquiring knowledge, skills, strategies, and understandings across various populations of learners and the full range of the subject matter. The number and variety of digital books are growing exponentially. Consequently, learning designers at all levels are required to become researchers and curators. They must find, analyze, and organize an ever-changing collection of learning materials suited to their purposes and drawn from an ever-expanding universe of possibilities.

The idea of learning designers—whether curriculum planners or classroom teachers—as digital curators is an important concept. Curation, mentioned in Chap. 11, often is spoken of in library contexts, but the vast availability of the learning matter on the Internet makes curation a role that all educators must adopt. In the words of school librarian Joyce Kasman Valenza (2012), "Digital curators can prevent oversaturation by filtering and diverting the onslaught and by directing what is worth sharing into more gentle and continuous streams."

The Book Format Decision Chart (Fig. 11.1) provides a simple rubric for considering format features that will best match learners' needs in the context of a given learning design. In this chapter, I explore some sources for digital texts that can be examined to determine whether they meet those needs.

D.R. Walling, *Designing Learning for Tablet Classrooms: Innovations in Instruction*, 69
DOI 10.1007/978-3-319-02420-2_12, © Springer International Publishing Switzerland 2014

12.2 Original Sources

In Chap. 10, I reviewed several options for finding digital reading matter related to literature study, including Project Gutenberg (http://www.gutenberg.org), which also offers free e-books in other subject categories, such as music, the sciences, fine arts, social studies, and so forth. The website lists 23 categories holding some 42,000 free books. This Internet site and others like it are ideal for locating original sources—in other words, historical texts. Most of these texts are free because the material is long out of copyright.

It should be borne in mind that the maxim "you get what you pay for" applies. Free digitized texts, often merely digital facsimiles of print, do not necessarily provide the features associated with more sophisticated e-reading, such as dictionary lookup, Web links, and searching. However, the type of features available also can depend on how the e-book is downloaded. For example, Louisa May Alcott's *Little Women* is available from Project Gutenberg in several formats. If it is downloaded to a Kindle app, then while the look of the text may not be as tidy as some paid e-books, the Kindle features still function. Text can be highlighted, dictionary lookup works, and so on.

Learning designers searching for e-books can check the Internet using "free ebooks" as a keyword. Adding "for kindle," "for nook," or "for android" can help refine the search. Another way to search is to include the subject descriptor in the keyword, such as "free science ebooks." Among the results for this last keyword, for instance, will be Science Books Online (http://www.sciencebooksonline.info). Books and articles on this website are organized in nine categories, from astronomy to physics, and the available texts include both historical works (e.g., Vernon L. Kellogg's *American Insects*, 1904) and more recent works (e.g., M.E. Cates' lecture notes on "Complex Fluids: The Physics of Emulsions," 2012). Many of the works can be read directly online using a tablet computer or downloaded as a PDF. The PDF often is a straightforward facsimile, purely text and whatever illustrations might have been included in the print edition. However, PDFs can be opened in different ways. If opened in iBooks on an iPad, for example, the reader will have access to standard iBooks PDF features, such as dictionary lookup. The features are not as numerous as for books in iBooks but are more than the reader will find when simply reading a PDF as digitized print pages.

12.3 Digital Libraries

An increasing number of libraries maintain digital holdings that they make available to patrons. In many communities, this applies to the local public library as well as nearby university libraries. And, of course, more and more school libraries are following suit. The Digital Age also is marked by expanding globalism, which means that digital library resources are not limited to geographic localities.

As an example, Cambridge University in England maintains a digital library on the Internet: ebooks@cambridge (http://www.lib.cam.ac.uk/ebooks/free.html). The free e-book collections encompass the arts, the humanities, social sciences, science, technology, medicine, and a miscellaneous category titled "multidisciplinary." Within the arts category, for instance, there is a link to open access e-books for film studies, which listed (as of July 2013) more than one hundred free e-books, most with copyright dates in the 1980s or more recently. For example, Nanna Verhoeff's 2012 book, *Mobile Screens: The Visual Regime of Navigation*, could be downloaded, complete with its color cover and various illustrations, as a PDF and then read through iBooks or a comparable Android app.

While Cambridge University's digital library is open to use without much effort, other e-book collections require logins or accounts. For example, the New York Public Library has a digital library website at eNYPL (http://ebooks.nypl.org). Patrons need to have an e-account—a library card or PIN—to log in and access the collection.

Another key difference between libraries like Cambridge and New York is resource usability. "Open access" at Cambridge allows users to download *and keep* the materials. The New York Public Library *lends* e-books, meaning that registered patrons may download an e-book only for a designated length of time. The eNYPL allows patrons to borrow up to a dozen digital titles, with the lending period varying from title to title. Lending periods often vary in accordance with the terms of agreements with publishers of digital content. Different publishers, therefore different terms.

In some cases, digital rights management (DRM) software is used to limit lending, downloading, and copying of e-books. DRM, digital copyright, and related matters remain controversial and, from both legal and logistical standpoints, are largely unresolved as yet. This is a consideration for learning designers to keep in mind as they look at ways to acquire reading matter to fulfill learning objectives.

12.4 Government Repositories

Government or quasi-government entities offer a great deal of freely available information, including a vast range of digital content. An excellent starting place for any learning designer seeking e-books or other digital texts is the Library of Congress (http://www.loc.gov). The library's Digital Collections and Services Department is a gateway into a trove of resources, particularly for readers interested in history, culture, government, journalism, and the arts. One of the subsites in this department is the American Memory collection. Designing a lesson on African American history and want to read what Frederick Douglass had to say? Go to The Frederick Douglass Papers (http://memory.loc.gov/ammem/doughtml/doughome.html) and download some of his writings, including his autobiography, published in 1855, *My Bondage and My Freedom*. Or perhaps it's a lesson on the great American sport of baseball and how it developed. The *Spalding Base Ball Guides, 1889–1939* will offer original source information about the sport. That's also in the American Memory collection.

Publications.USA.gov (http://publications.usa.gov) is fairly user-friendly and offers digital reading matter on numerous subjects. This website is a function of the Federal Citizen Information Center (FCIC) and functions similar to a repository for materials from various government entities. For example, readers who find a short, free e-book on *Back Yard Bird Feeding* will actually be linked to U.S. Fish and Wildlife Service (http://library.fws.gov) Conservation Library to read it online. In another instance, site users who find *The New Wave in Electronics: eCycling* can directly download a PDF of this free pamphlet without following a link to its originator. Many of the materials listed on this website are brief and consumer-oriented and so may be more useful in earlier grades than some of the more challenging historical texts from the Library of Congress.

NASA (the National Aeronautics and Space Administration) also offers a number of free e-books through its Connect website (http://www.nasa.gov/connect/ebooks/index.html). As would be expected, most concern topics related to aviation and space. But it's not all about just technology. For example, there is *Earth as Art,* satellite views of our planet, which is a downloadable PDF. An accompanying iPad app also can be downloaded from the NASA site. Most of the e-books are available in several formats: EPUB, MOBI, PDF, and iBook. All are free of charge.

12.5   Commercial Sources

While many digital texts are available without charge, there are additional resource websites where e-books can be purchased. One is the U.S. Government Bookstore (http://bookstore.gpo.gov/ebooks), which offers e-books mainly for sale. Users of the website can browse by topic or government department. *2011 The FBI Story,* for example, is published by the Department of Justice and is available as an e-book for less than $10. This title and other e-books can be obtained through a linked third-party e-book seller, either Apple iBook Store (which requires an iTunes account) or the Google Play eBook Store.

These two third-party sellers for the U.S. Government Bookstore, of course, are excellent starting points in themselves. Apple iBooks are sold through iTunes (preview at http://itunes.apple.com/us/app/ibooks/id364709193?mt=8). Within the iBooks app for the iPad, users can visit the online bookstore to search for titles that can then be downloaded directly to the tablet device.

Google Play (http://play.google.com) offers several subcategories: music, books, magazines, movies and TV, Android apps, and devices. The digital books category functions like most online booksellers. e-Books can be downloaded directly to a tablet device. Some are paid downloads, some are free; and soon-to-be-published books can be preordered.

While the iBook Store and Google Play are commercial booksellers, both sites offer many free e-books. Most, as expected, are older, out-of-copyright works.

Amazon.com (http://www.amazon.com) provides access to a vast number of e-books through links on its Free eBooks: Collections page (simply search on "amazon.com free ebooks"). The listed collections include Amazon's own Kindle Store (popular classics), Internet Archive (millions of titles, mainly accessed through historical collections), Open Library (more than a million free titles), Project Gutenberg (mentioned previously), and ManyBooks.net (more than 26,000 free titles). So, even though Amazon.com is the world's largest commercial online bookseller, interested learning designers can find an array of free digital content that can be tapped to develop lessons on virtually any topic.

12.6 Summary

Learning designers can tap a myriad of sources for digital reading matter for students at all levels and abilities and for all of the subjects across the broadest curriculum. The mix of sources is rich and growing richer daily. Many, as would be expected, are commercial websites offering e-books and other materials for a price. In this chapter, however, I have highlighted an array of options for obtaining free texts. They include Internet-based archives and digital libraries—and even a few commercial booksellers.

The challenge for learning designers, from curriculum developers to classroom teachers, is to find, analyze, and organize the materials best suited to their needs and the needs of their students. This is digital curation, and it can seem like an overwhelming challenge. Today's digital curators must hone their investigative skills, using keywords like scalpels to cut through the mass of available information right to the heart of what they need.

One of the sources mentioned earlier is Internet Archive (http://archive.org), with the motto, "universal access to all knowledge." That sounds like an exaggeration until one notes that the website is a gateway to more than 4.6 million texts. Many of these are freely available for tablet applications, such as Nook, Kindle, iBooks, and PDF. This abundance has changed the equation for learning design. Today it isn't so much a matter of finding enough reading matter for tablet-mediated learning; it's a matter of deciding what to include in the learning design.

Reference

Valenza, J. K. (2012, September-October). Curation. *School Library monthly* 29. Retrieved July 9, 2013, from http://www.schoollibrarymonthly.com/articles/Valenza2012-v29n1p20.html

Chapter 13
Are Apps a Good Fit for Learning Goals?

13.1 Introduction

New software applications, or apps, for tablet computers seem to be created every day. That's probably no exaggeration. The statistics keep growing. Early in 2012, for example, Apple's vice president for marketing announced that there were then some 20,000 education apps for the iPad—and more than 1.5 million iPads in schools and other education institutions (Rad, 2012). Although the iPad is the leading tablet computer, there are many others and the number of education apps for those is exploding as well.

Many apps have high potential as teaching and learning tools—but are they a good fit for a specific learning design? That's the real question, just as it is the same question pursued in previous chapters with regard to e-books and eTextbooks. In Chaps. 11 and 12, I identified the concept of digital curation with regard to finding, analyzing, and organizing digital texts. That concept extends to all learning media, including apps. But, in fact, curation may be more nuanced when it comes to applications for tablet computers.

A key difference between digital texts and apps is that multimedia components can make some apps more like games. It can be tempting to "automate" instruction, but that can be like parking a toddler in front of a television, aka a one-eyed babysitter. Sometimes, of course, within a larger design for learning, independent app use is entirely appropriate. So, what makes an app a good fit? This chapter examines characteristics and criteria to keep in mind when choosing and using tablet apps for teaching and learning.

D.R. Walling, *Designing Learning for Tablet Classrooms: Innovations in Instruction*, DOI 10.1007/978-3-319-02420-2_13, © Springer International Publishing Switzerland 2014

13.2 Blended or Flipped?

Two of the current buzzwords in schools today are *blended learning* and *flipped classrooms*. *Blended learning* refers to blending online and traditional teaching and learning. That's a very broad definition for a very broad concept. There is no dividing line where a traditional approach merely supplemented by online resources becomes "blended." *Keeping Pace with K-12 Online and Blended Learning* (Watson, Murin, Vashaw, Gemin & Rapp, 2012), an annual publication of the Evergreen Education Group since 2004, focuses primarily, though not exclusively, on the incorporation of online courses in the standard school curriculum, but the term *blended learning* often is applied more generically to learning designs that include online (or even simply digital) learning in otherwise traditional education settings. *Keeping Pace* also refers to this general notion, citing the Innosight Institute definition: "A formal education program in which a student learns at least in part through online delivery of content and instruction with some element of student control over time, place, path, and/or pace, and at least in part at a supervised brick-and-mortar location away from home" (p. 7). Blended learning runs the gamut, therefore, from incidental inclusion of online learning vehicles in traditional classrooms to fully Internet-based learning, often called cyberschools.

For learning designers developing designs for tablet classrooms, the idea of blended learning usually finds iteration in the supplemental use of online learning vehicles integrated with traditional classroom instruction.

Let's consider Kahn Academy (http://www.khanacademy.org), a widely used instructional video source. Kahn Academy videos—more than 4,200—offer self-paced instruction in a wide range of subjects for a broad K-12+ audience. Teachers who formally incorporate the videos into their classroom learning designs can obtain information about individual student and whole-class performance. Most of the videos are only 10 min long and are designed for independent viewing on virtually any computer.

This resource is important in the consideration of tablet apps because in March 2012 Kahn Academy launched an iPad app that can be downloaded without charge (http://www.khanacademy.org/about/blog/post/24905749288/ipad-app). The app allows users to view any of the videos available from the Kahn Academy website. A feature that may be even more important, especially for classrooms with rationed Internet access or for students who take their iPads to homes that do not have wireless access, is that the videos can be downloaded for offline viewing. (This is exactly how most e-books work. Once downloaded, the user does not need to be connected to the Internet to use the resource.) A similar Android app also is available, but the reviews to date have been mixed.

The *flipped classroom* is a variation of blended learning. Rather than the teacher spending class time on direct instruction or lecture, the students view online lectures or demonstrations, usually on their own time or as homework. Class time is then devoted to hands-on learning, such as discussing key questions, solving problems, or tackling projects. Proponents tout the advantages of more hands-on learning during teacher-contact time, which may better align with a constructivist view of teaching and learning. However, detractors point out that the success of this flipped approach is predicated on students being both willing to learn independently and capable of doing so as an initial approach to the subject matter at hand.

According to the authors of a Flipped Learning Network (http://www.flippedlearning.org) report, four "pillars" support effective flipped learning: a flexible environment in which students engage fully (and sometimes noisily); a cultural shift toward student-centered learning from teacher-centered instruction; intentional content that supports active learning strategies during class time; and professional educators, recognizing that online, independent learning cannot replace effective teacher-student interaction in school (Hamdan, McKnight, McKnight, & Arfstrom, 2013).

The Kahn Academy videos, whether viewed at school or elsewhere, can be effective in the context of a flipped classroom approach to learning design. The same is true for a number of apps, which can be used independently in a flipped learning approach.

Tablet classrooms are inherently blended learning environments. So the question really is more than, are apps a good fit? Rather, learning designers need to consider a twofold question: Which apps are a good fit for which purposes, and when should such apps be used?

13.3 Critical Questions for Using Apps

Tablet apps for education tend to serve one or more of three functions: introduce subject matter, supplement instruction, or reinforce learning. Many do all three. For learning designers of every sort, the choices about whether and when to use a particular app need to be based on criteria that speak to suitability and circumstance. Is the app right for *this* purpose at *this* time? Given the overwhelming number of available apps, it can be a challenge to find and evaluate those apps that are the best fit for a particular learning design. Following are four critical questions that can help chart a path through the dense app jungle.

What is the app intended to do? This sounds almost simplistic, but apps are developed for a purpose (or a set of purposes). Reading the developer's notes therefore can be a starting point. Does the app developer's intention match the goal of the learning design? But this question needs to go further, to be a little nuanced. Is the subject matter conveyed in a positive manner? Does it use effective modeling of learning? In other words, the app needs to be in character with the learning design, not merely a superficial match in terms of subject matter.

How is the app intended to be used? If an app is designed to be used independently, it is likely to be a better choice for a flipped learning situation, for instance, than an app specifically designed to reinforce previously introduced concepts. Considering this question can help the learning designer place the app to the best advantage—before, during, or after addressing the target subject matter in class.

Embedded in this question is one focused on ease of use. If an app is designed to be used when the teacher is not around, is it easy for students to use without help?

Is the app age and ability appropriate? Most app developers aim for a target user age, but sometimes the age range is unrealistically broad. The question really should center on developmental, rather than chronological, age. For the learning designer, is this app right for this student or this particular group of students? Appropriateness in this context also extends to considering the student user's physical abilities or limitations. Is the app compatible with, or adaptable to address, vision or hearing impairments, dexterity limitations, or other conditions that require accommodation?

Is the app engaging? Most apps are made for one-on-one engagement by the user, and so the question of appropriateness also needs to go beyond whether the student *can* use the app to whether the student will *want* to use it. For apps to be used outside the classroom, this is especially important. The flipped classroom works only when students engage with subject matter on their own as well as when they are in a classroom setting.

13.4   Review Assistance

The critical questions in the preceding section need to be the basis for reviewing apps to use with students. There may be additional questions, depending on the learning design or other circumstances. Common considerations include price, value, and privacy. "Here's the problem," writes Tanya Roscoria (2013) for the Center for Digital Education, "Teachers don't have much time to sift through thousands of apps and figure out how they'll work in the classroom."

Reviews help learning designers winnow the educationally valuable apps from the clutter of digital choices. Fortunately, there are a number of reliable review services. Following, in no particular order, is a sampling to illustrate their range:

eSchool News (http://www.eschoolnews.com) bills itself as "Technology News for Today's K-20 Educator" and often publishes "10 best" or similar app roundups. Interested persons can subscribe to a free e-newsletter.

eCampus News (http://www.ecampusnews.com) is the higher education counterpart to eSchool News, with a website and free e-newsletters along the same lines.

Edudemic (http://www.edudemic.com), which has a stated goal "to connect teachers, administrators, students, and just about everyone else with the best technology on the planet," regularly publishes "best apps" features. These reviews are archived under "The Best of EdTech" on their homepage.

Edutopia (http://www.edutopia.org), founded by filmmaker George Lucas, is "dedicated to improving the K-12 learning process by documenting, disseminating, and advocating innovative, replicable, and evidence-based strategies that prepare students to thrive in their future education, careers, and adult lives." The site publishes reviews of apps and related articles.

Best Education Apps (http://www.besteducationalapps.com), as the name implies, is wholly dedicated to reviewing education apps in a wide range of categories. The focus tends to lean somewhat toward the younger—elementary through middle school—grade range.

Educational Technology and Mobile Learning (http://www.educatorstechnology.com) is the website of a Canadian educator, Med Kharbach, who collates and publishes app reviews.

Appolicious (http://www.appolicious.com) bills itself as "a mobile app discovery service." The site is not dedicated specifically to education, but users will find reviews of many education apps for early childhood through high school.

An Internet search using the keywords "best education apps" or a modification for specifics, such as "apps for iPad" or "apps for science," will yield a number of additional sources of reviews and other information, everything from random newspaper articles to personal blogs.

Common Sense Media (http://www.commonsensemedia.org), dedicated "to improving the lives of kids and families" through trustworthy information and education, has launched a new Web platform for educators called Graphite (http://www.graphite.org). Created with funding from Bill Gates, the Microsoft magnate turned philanthropist, Graphite is dedicated to building a "dynamic community" of teachers "sharing their personal reviews and field notes about how they use specific websites, games, and apps, and what works best with their students." In other words, Graphite offers the equivalent of a digital peer review system to identify apps and other media that really work.

Users of the Graphite website can search for app reviews by school subject, grade (prekindergarten to 12), price (free, free to try, or paid), and device (iPad, Android, etc.). If the site grows as intended, it should be a valuable help to learning designers as they attempt to sort through thousands of educational apps to find (à la Goldilocks) those that are just right.

13.5 Summary

Are apps a good fit for learning goals? The answer probably is yes simply because there are so many available applications for tablet computers that there's bound to be one that fits a particular learning design. Ensuring that good fit is another matter. One key question involves determining which apps are a good fit for specific learning designs. By the inclusion of tablet computers as central devices, tablet classrooms are naturally blended learning environments. But getting the blend of traditional and technological approaches to teaching and learning just right is the central curatorial challenge.

A second key question centers on determining when to incorporate apps into learning designs. A flipped learning approach might be best achieved by using an app as a launch pad—that is, having students use an app independently as an introduction or grounding before the teacher expands on the lesson in class, through demonstrations, discussions, projects, and other approaches. In other situations, the more effective placement of an app might be later in the lesson, for practice or reinforcement of learned content. Given a growing and already seemingly endless variety of learning apps available for tablet computers of all sorts, there is likely to be a solution that fits every type of learning design. Thus, the real challenge is curatorial.

Meeting this challenge means examining the four critical questions outlined in this chapter: What is the app intended to do? How is the app intended to be used? Is the app appropriate? Is the app engaging? Fortunately, many review services exist to help learning designers at all levels of education find those 5 or 10 or 15 "best" apps for whatever purpose they need. Still, it should be remembered that even the best of the services merely provides a starting point. Ultimately, it is up to the learning designer to curate app resources, to make informed judgments about apps in the same way that teachers and curriculum developers have always had to make judgments about appropriate learning resources since students read from papyrus and parchment.

References

Hamdan N., McKnight, P., McKnight, K., & Arfstrom, K. M. (2013) *A review of flipped learning.* Arlington, VA: Flipped Learning Network. http://www.flippedlearning.org

Rad, L. (2012, January 19) Apple: 20,000 education iPad apps developed; 1.5 million devices in use at schools. *TE.* Retrieved July 12, 2013, from http://techcrunch.com/2012/01/19/apple-20000-education-ipad-apps-developed-1-5-million-devices-in-use-at-schools/

Roscoria, T. (2013, July 2) The problem with apps in school. *Center for Digital Education.* Retrieved July 24, 2013, from http://www.centerdigitaled.com/news/The-Problem-with-Apps-in-School.html

Watson, J., Murin, A., Vashaw, L., Gemin, B., & Rapp, C. (2012) *2012 keeping pace with K-12 online and blended learning.* Durango, CO: Evergreen Education Group. http://kpk12.com

Chapter 14
The Immediacy of Connectivity: Pluses and Pitfalls

14.1 Introduction

In wired classrooms, tablet computers can give students and teachers immediate connectivity to the Internet—provided that the institution has adequate Wi-Fi capabilities and policies that permit access. Connectivity can open a door to a myriad of information and education resources. But connectivity comes with a price that is not measured only in dollars and cents. In the vast sea of the Internet, there are sharks.

Learning designers as well as information technology (IT) specialists, managers, and administrators in education institutions at all levels must navigate these waters in ways that avoid the most egregious perils, from sites that pander pornography to those simply purveying unreliable information, from lurkers to bullies. How can learning designers best construct learning situations to capitalize on the dynamic potential of Internet resources while avoiding trouble spots?

There is a well-worn concept often repeated by motivational speakers that the Chinese word for *crisis* is composed of symbols for *danger* and *opportunity*. Internet connectivity frequently is seen by educators and policy makers as a crisis just waiting to happen. Indeed, there are perils—dangers, if you will, or sharks, to extend the previous metaphor—lurking beneath the glistening surface of connectivity. But there also are many opportunities for teachers and students to construct knowledge and understandings, to create learning.

This chapter presents a summary of five opportunities and concomitant challenges of connectivity, from the technical to the intellectual, and includes suggestions for dealing with them. Doubtless, there are more than five, but these are the ones most often significant, first, for institutions, whether K-12 or higher education, and, second, for learning designers who want students to use resources on the Internet. Learning designers who become savvy about what the Web has to offer for educational purposes will find that they hold the keys to a treasury of resources.

D.R. Walling, *Designing Learning for Tablet Classrooms: Innovations in Instruction*, 81
DOI 10.1007/978-3-319-02420-2_14, © Springer International Publishing Switzerland 2014

14.2   Connectivity

The first opportunity/challenge is simply how best to achieve connectivity that is reliable, powerful, and, for all intents and purposes, universal—at least, throughout the institution. This is a technology infrastructure issue. The magic word is *bandwidth*, essentially the capacity of a network to transmit data. In general, nontechnical terms, the more bandwidth a network has, the more data it can carry and the faster that data can be transmitted. Many schools and universities are struggling to increase their networks' bandwidth to meet the ever-increasing demands for widespread 24/7 access to the Internet. But this also is a moment of opportunity. Funds follow focus. As the need for reliable, high-speed connectivity increases, it is given higher funding priority.

Testing requirements in K-12 education related to the Common Core State Standards that have been adopted in many states recently raised school infrastructure issues to new heights of both interest and concern. Spring 2013 saw a parade of headlines trumpeting problems with connectivity during many schools' attempts to implement online testing as part of the Common Core requirements. Schools across the United States found that they lacked the bandwidth or had other technological limitations that became evident when large numbers of students went online for testing. According to *Education Week*, "Thousands of students experienced slow loading times of test questions, students were closed out of testing in mid-answer, and some were unable to log in to the tests" (Davis, 2013). Some of the problems were traced back to the testing companies; others clearly were related to or exacerbated by institutional infrastructure limitations.

Most learning designers cannot directly solve infrastructure problems, but they can serve as advisors. As tablet classrooms proliferate and more and more students need access to the Internet as a basic learning tool, learning designers can be the leading advocates for ramping up their institutions' technology infrastructures to ensure maximum connectivity for teaching and learning.

14.3   Reliable Information

Connectivity offers access to an abundance of information that is impossible for most learning institutions to achieve with bricks and mortar. "Technology-based approaches to learning," according to Australian researchers Ron Oliver and Jan Herrington, "provide many opportunities for constructivist learning through their provision and support for resource-based, student-centered settings and by enabling learning to be related to context and to practice" (2003, p. 12). Online resources thus allow learning designers to develop flexible approaches to content acquisition, rather than spend time creating or assembling content. This opportunity to focus less on content and more on learning strategies and activities permits learning designers to give greater attention to students' construction of knowledge and understandings.

In the words of Oliver and Herrington, "In learning environments that support knowledge construction, learners need to be exposed to a variety of resources and to have choices in the resources that they use and how they use them" (p. 15). Connectivity offers a cornucopia of choices.

The challenge is discerning which information is trustworthy. This challenge has always existed, and teachers have always needed to help their students examine resources with a critical eye. Is the source scholarly or popular? Is the author a recognized authority? Is the information current, complete, valid, objective, and so on? The Internet has introduced a new aspect. All of these questions are still valid for Internet resources, but now, there are some new questions because Web-based content may be or, at first glance, may seem to be anonymous. Can it still be trustworthy?

Learning designers now must incorporate a new set of critical considerations to help students identify reliable information on the Internet. For example, one easy-to-teach strategy is to help students parse URLs to identify sources of information. A first clue to whether a website is potentially trustworthy is its domain extension. The most common extensions are .gov (government), .edu (education), .org (organization, usually though no longer exclusively nonprofit), and .com (commercial). The last of these domains usually demands the most scrutiny—but not necessarily. For example, the *New York Times* online is a commercial website (http://www.nytimes.com). But the newspaper has a reputation for reliability. So simply being a commercial enterprise does not make a source suspect.

A useful resource for teaching this strategy and others is "Evaluating Web Pages: Techniques to Apply and Questions to Ask" from the University of California, Berkeley (2012). Another excellent resource for learning designers is a *CQ Researcher* report titled "Internet Accuracy" (2008).

14.4 Security

In the context of this list, security refers to devices and software. Connectivity opens a conduit through which many bits of data flow. Most bits are useful or at least neutral. However, some are hazardous. Learning designers need to work with IT personnel to ensure that potential disruption or damage is not caused by a teacher or a student accidentally downloading a virus. Viruses can infect individual computers and entire networks. Like human viruses, they can be nasty and hard to get rid of. Most districts have protocols in place to avoid viruses, such as antivirus-scanning programs that warn about potentially damaging downloads or block certain types of websites. (This type of blocking is different from filtering software that blocks types of content, as discussed later in this list.) Some learning designs also incorporate the use of online interpersonal communication, using email or online chatting. Like antivirus programs, spam filters help keep unwanted communication from intruding on lessons.

The opportunity associated with this topic is to help students learn how to use their devices to access information freely while being conscious of security issues. Such basic technology-use lessons, incorporated into learning designs as needed, will be valuable to students not only in school but also as they use tablets, smartphones, and other devices at home, in a future workplace, or elsewhere. Learning designers should consider incorporating basic security tips and strategies whenever students are introduced to online learning, whether the students' activities involve conducting searches for information or taking an interactive online course.

The U.S. Department of Homeland Security hosts a cyber-security tips page: US-CERT (United States Computer Emergency Readiness Team) at https://www.us-cert.gov/ncas/tips. The site offers information about "common security issues for non-technical computer users," from protecting portable devices to dealing with cyberbullies. This latter area relates to the next challenge: safety.

14.5   Safety

Connectivity on a personal level often centers on one-to-one communication, using email or chatting in some form. Texting using a mobile phone is a form of chatting and is the predominant form of electronic communication for young people. In fact, there's an age-demographic divide. According to one study of email versus text message, users aged 13–25 clearly favored texting, while users aged 39 and older favored emailing (AARP, 2012). Users of the iPad, incidentally, will have noticed that the keyboard can be split, configuring it for thumb-typing that is characteristic of texting on smaller mobile devices, such as smartphones. Google's Nexus tablets and others offer a similar feature.

Increasingly, chatting is being incorporated into learning designs. Writing for the website Education World, associate editor Jason Tomaszewski (2012) comments, "Capitalizing on students' fascination with texting and other digital communication, well-implemented electronic chats can support their critical thinking, in addition to building knowledge through 'social constructivism.'"

A number of Web-based chat sites are potentially useful in learning designs that call for electronic communication among students, such as Chatzy (http://www.chatzy.com) and, to make international connections, Kidlink (http://www.kidlink.org). They function equally well on most devices, from desktop computers to smartphones. Both allow educators to set up chat rooms with admission by invitation only. This is an important consideration, regardless of the age of the students.

Tablet apps for chat also are available, including apps that go beyond the simple chat platform. An example of the latter is RabbleBrowser, from Float Mobile Learning (http://floatlearning.com/mobile-learning-apps/rabblebrowser/#.UfkzHhZhwc8). RabbleBrowser facilitates sharing a Web-browsing experience. A leader (teacher or student) curates the experience, sharing URLs and files. Invited participants can discuss ideas, view demonstrations, and engage in the interactions whether they are physically in the same classroom or scattered in various locations.

The ability to limit participation or curate connected online activities is essential. One of the major safety challenges of Internet connectivity is the potential for cyberbullying, or the use of technology to harass, threaten, or stalk individuals.

Cyberbullying affects students of all ages, from elementary school to university. Because schools expose students to the Internet, it falls to learning designers to assist in measures to prevent or curb cyberbullying. While cyberbullies can target anyone, sexual minority students often are singled out, as are students perceived not to "fit in" in some way.

Readers may recall, for example, that September 2010 was a deadly month to be young and gay. On September 9, Billy Lucas, a 15-year-old from Greensburg, Indiana, hanged himself from a barn rafter after a constant barrage of antigay bullying at school. Two weeks later, on September 23, Asher Brown, a 13-year-old eighth grader who had come out to his parents after being bullied at school, shot himself in his Houston suburb. On September 28, Seth Walsh died after spending a week on life support in Tehachapi, California. The 13-year-old hanged himself in his backyard after suffering relentless taunting and abuse at school (Badash, 2010).

University students also were affected. Tyler Clementi, an 18-year-old Rutgers University student, jumped off the George Washington Bridge on September 28, days after his roommate allegedly posted a video on the Internet of Clementi having sex with another man. And on September 29, Raymond Chase, an openly gay 19-year-old at Johnson and Wales University in Providence, Rhode Island, hanged himself in his dorm room (Badash, 2010).

In two of these five cases, the impetus for suicide is uncertain, but in the other three cases, there is no question that antigay bullying drove these adolescents to end their lives. At least some, if not most, of that bullying was carried out over the Internet.

Learning designers necessarily need to be cognizant of the potential safety risks whenever online interpersonal communication is a feature of the learning design, particularly in instances when students may be contacted by someone they do not know.

The education website Science Buddies offers a useful "Internet Safety Guide" at http://www.sciencebuddies.org/science-fair-projects/project_ideas/Internet_Safety. shtml. The guide, underwritten by the cyber security company Symantec, offers guidelines covering identity, e-mailing, social networking, blogging, downloading, and related topics for educators working with K-12 students, but the principles are applicable for all Internet users. After the incidents of September 2010, the federal government also ramped up its information service on cyberbullying, which is online at http://www.stopbullying.gov.

14.6 Appropriate Content

All Internet users, regardless of age, eventually will stumble onto websites that they consider inappropriate for themselves or their students or children. Learning designers who incorporate Internet connectivity in lesson activities need to consider students' experience with the Internet to determine whether to include instruction about avoiding inappropriate content. Often, the introduction of Internet-connected learning activities provides an opportunity to help students become more Internet-savvy, which will serve them well in the long term. Conducting proactive education about the Internet—including specific guidance about what is and isn't appropriate in the lesson context at hand—and setting ground rules for Internet use, such as always using tablets in a shared setting where screens are visible to others, are positive approaches.

"Inappropriate" often is construed as "adult" (usually pornographic), but some Internet content is simply time wasting. Games that are not part of the lesson design, for example, can be addictive and consume valuable time better spent on learning activities. Ensuring that content is on topic will help keep learning on target—and it will contribute to correcting a misimpression among many parents that what their students get from the Internet and mobile apps in school is "purely entertainment." The latter was a finding in a study by Grunwald Associates (2013).

Another way that learning designers can help students avoid inappropriate content is by providing starting points, such as websites related to learning content that contain links that students can use to propel their own Internet searches in productive and appropriate directions. Common Sense Media (http://www.commonsensemedia.org), mentioned in Chap. 13, is one of a number of review sites that can provide information for learning designers to use in constructing lessons that rely on Internet connectivity.

Finally, a number of Internet filters are available to limit content availability. "Parent controls," as they are often called, restrict students' ability to view certain websites. Depending on the filtering program, the software also may be capable of monitoring chat, blocking social networking, blocking games, and reporting search activities. Tablets are a relatively new form of computer, and filtering software and apps at the device level are fairly basic but being improved, particularly as more schools move toward tablet classrooms.

However, filtering in education settings is primarily done at the network (school district or university) level. The difficulty with most Internet filters is that they eliminate access with a cleaver rather than a scalpel. The filtering mechanisms differ with the network software. Blocking commonly is based on URLs, keywords, or blacklists. Sites with appropriate content can get blocked along with inappropriate sites. A 2012 report from the American Association of School Librarians noted that filtering most often blocked websites for teachers and other staff as well as for students in most K-12 settings. In the survey on which the report was based, 52 % of respondents said that filtering "impeded student research when topic or keyword searches are filtered." However, half of the respondents also said that filtering "decreased the potential number of distractions" (AASL, 2012). Most districts have override policies to circumvent overzealous filtering software, but the override can take a day or two to implement.

14.7   Summary

Previous chapters have included discussions of digital content, tablet apps, and uses of tablet computers that do not necessarily rely on "live" connectivity. The target device need only to have been connected to the Internet long enough to download the content or the applications. The accessibility of app functions and digital texts when tablets are offline is indispensible for times when having students' devices connected to the Internet is not possible, such as when they use their tablets out of Wi-Fi range or when bandwidth limitations make 24/7 connectivity for all users impossible. Out-of-Wi-Fi-range capabilities maintain key tablet functionality when students use their tablets in homes without Internet connectivity, on field trips, or outdoors. It's still possible to read an e-book under a tree in the park or take notes during a trip to a museum.

However, connectivity offers many additional opportunities because the Internet is a trove of potential learning. Blended learning and flipped classrooms, discussed in Chap. 13, are not feasible without effective connectivity. But every opportunity comes with challenges, whether they are related to achieving connectivity, discerning reliable information, maintaining security and safety, or ensuring that content is appropriate. Ultimately, the challenge for learning designers is to navigate the uncertain seas of Internet connectivity to achieve optimal teaching and learning.

References

AARP. (2012). *Connecting generations.* Washington, DC: AARP Research & Strategic Analysis. http://www.aarp.org

AASL (American Association of School Librarians). (2012). *2012 School libraries count! Supplemental report on filtering.* Chicago, IL: AASL. http://www.ala.org

Badash, D. (2010, October 1). UPDATED: September's anti-gay bullying suicides—There were a lot more than 5. *New civil rights movement.* Retrieved July 30, 2013, from http://thenewcivil-rightsmovement.com/septembers-anti-gay-bullying-suicides-there-were-a-lot-more-than-5/discrimination/2010/10/01/13297

CQ Researcher. (August 1, 2008). Internet accuracy. *CQ Researcher* 18. 625–648. http://www.cqpress.com

Davis, M. R. (2013, May 7). States' online testing problems raise common-core concerns. *Education Week.* Retrieved July 30, 2013, from http://www.edweek.org/ew/articles/2013/05/03/30testing.h32.html?tkn=NQLFTwp25lEd71ZsCXwVwwKXX%2BmeW LE%2FIUj2&cmp=ENL-EU-NEWS1

Grunwald Associates. (2013). *Living and learning with mobile devices: What parents think about mobile devices for early childhood and K–12 learning.* San Francisco, CA: Author.

Oliver, R., & Herrington, J. (2003). Exploring technology-mediated learning from a pedagogical perspective. *Journal of Interactive Learning Environments, 11,* 111–126.

Tomaszewski, J. Online chat: Ideas for classroom use. *Education World, 2012.* Retrieved July 31, 2013, from http://www.educationworld.com/a_tech/chat-room-get-new-life-in-classrooms.shtml

University of California Berkeley. (2012). Evaluating web pages: Techniques to apply and questions to ask from *Finding Information on the Internet: A Tutorial.* Berkeley: University of California. http://www.lib.berkeley.edu/TeachingLib/Guides/Internet/Evaluate.html

Chapter 15
Using Tablet Technology for Multisensory Learning

15.1 Introduction

Because vision tends to be the dominant human sense, at least in the Western world, learning designs often focus largely on the visual—text and images—without sufficiently recognizing that some students learn best through other senses, such as hearing and touch or movement. Tablet technology readily allows teachers to use multisensory learning strategies, from apps that capitalize on the touchscreen technology and provide tactile/kinesthetic learning to audio technology capable of recording and producing spoken words and music.

The idea of multisensory learning draws on theories of multiple intelligences and learning styles. Neither are novel theories at this point, though both still evoke debate. Practicing educators, parents, and others who work in learning situations with children and adolescents, or even adults, know firsthand that individuals learn in many different ways. For learning designers, the challenge is to engage as many sensory channels as possible in order to accommodate the varied ways that students acquire knowledge and understanding.

Multisensory learning strategies and tablet technology also are key to working effectively with students with sensory disabilities. Tablets are inherently assistive devices, and adaptive features that are not already built in to most tablets can be added on, by using apps and after-market or companion tools.

The purpose of this chapter is to explore facets of multisensory learning in the context of learning design for tablet classrooms.

15.2 Multiple Intelligences and Learning Styles

Harvard developmental psychologist Howard Gardner proposed his theory of multiple intelligences (MI) in a 1983 book titled, *Frames of Mind: The Theory of Multiple Intelligences*. Gardner's idea is that individuals' pathways to learning follow certain identifiable modalities, or "intelligences." In the 1980s, this proposition contradicted the prevailing notion that intelligence is a single quality of mind. Most modalities align with sensory experiences. Originally, Gardner proposed seven intelligences:

- Musical—rhythmic
- Visual—spatial
- Verbal—linguistic
- Logical—mathematical
- Bodily—kinesthetic
- Interpersonal
- Intrapersonal

In later writings, Gardner added naturalistic and existential intelligences, and other writers have suggested additions and adaptations that need not be considered here. Suffice to say, this perspective finds resonance in learning theories and practices—particularly constructivism. Gardner himself has taken up the educational ramifications in various ways over the course of his career. For the thirtieth anniversary reissue of *Frames of Mind*, Gardner provided a new introduction, in which he suggested not only using multiple intelligences theory to individualize learning experiences but also to "pluralize" learning. Pluralizing, according to Gardner, involves teachers and learning designers in many contexts prioritizing topics or concepts and then presenting them in a variety of ways. According to Gardner:

> Pluralization achieves two important goals: when a topic is taught in multiple ways, one reaches more students. Additionally, the multiple modes of delivery convey what it means to understand something well. When one has a thorough understanding of a topic, one can typically think of it in several ways, thereby making use of one's multiple intelligences. Conversely, if one is restricted to a single mode of conceptualization and presentation, one's own understanding is likely to be tenuous. (2011, p. 7)

Both of Gardner's goals in this suggestion find iteration throughout this chapter. The same can be said of another approach to multiplicity in learning: learning style theory. Unlike MI, no dominant figure has emerged in learning style theory; consequently, there are a variety of style theories and approaches. David Kolb's (1984) model of information processing often is used as a starting point. Kolb offers a useful perspective, namely, that learners need to become proficient in recognizing how they learn best. He writes:

> By developing their effectiveness as learners…students can be empowered to take responsibility for their own learning by understanding how they learn best and the skills necessary to learn in regions that are uncomfortable for them. (2005, p. 209)

This idea strongly resonates with the constructivist notions underpinning this book. Ultimately, learning styles tend to be distilled into four modalities:

- Visual
- Aural/auditory
- Reading/writing
- Kinesthetic/tactile

These broad categories identify individuals' preferred ways to approach and acquire information. Some years ago, as a teacher of writing, I became concerned that most writing instructions were conducted as though all students learned best through a reading/writing style. While this seems logical as a learning design approach for teaching writing, in my experience, it does not accommodate many students' actual learning modalities. My goal, therefore, in *Teaching Writing to Visual, Auditory, and Kinesthetic Learners* (Walling, 2006) was to suggest that learning designs can approach the teaching of composition—though it is inherently reading/writing—in alternative ways to better match the learning styles of students for whom a reading/writing style is an ill fit.

Multiple intelligences theory and learning style theories, despite long, practical use in classrooms, not only in the United States but in many other parts of the education world, are still contested. Critics point to a lack of proof, of empirical research in both cases. But, after all, that is the nature of theory. Most rational theories—theories that are largely confirmed by practice and observation—are at least tentatively adopted *during* the search for proof or until they can be proven wrong. Darwin's theory of evolution, for example, remains to be conclusively proven, although a great deal of evidence in support of the theory has accumulated. Most scientists act as though the theory is correct, absent conclusive proof that it is not, even as it continues to be hotly debated.

So, it is with theories of multiple intelligences and learning styles. In their broadest outlines, they make sense. They resonate with educators' and observers' experiences with learners, including themselves. Learning designers can draw on these ideas without being wedded to the nuances or being drawn into the debate over whether they have been sufficiently researched. These theories are philosophical rather than scientific—at least from the standpoint of learning design, which is as much about art as it is about science.

15.3   Multisensory Tablet Functionality

Tablet computers are up-sized smartphones without the phone function. Most students (77 % of 12- to 17-year-olds) at this time do not own personal tablet computers, but increasing numbers are learning in schools and classrooms that supply tablets. One reason that tablets are catching on so quickly is that they are an immediate "fit" for young people. This is where the comparison to smartphones is important. According to Pew Research, 78 % of teens (ages 12–17) have cell phones. As of 2012, 37 % of all teens have smartphones, up from only 23 % in 2011, a scant year earlier. Among teens with smartphones, fully half report using their phones as the main way they access the Internet (Madden et al., 2013). All of these figures appear to be on a steep rise as time goes on.

Tablet computers are an easy transition from devices that many students already use, and for others, it usually is a quick learning curve. This is one reason that it is simplistic to view the tablet device itself—a high-tech toy to some critics—as the main draw.

Interest more likely derives from functionality and is sustained by student interaction with the device's features. Susan Linn for the Campaign for a Commercial-Free Childhood is opposed to electronic toys, in general but for the very youngest learners in particular. Her notion is, "The best toy is 10 % toy and 90 % child" (Szabo, 2011). Philosophically, I agree; and the notion should apply to learning tools of all sorts for students of all ages. Tablet computers are not merely high-tech toys. They are toolboxes for learner engagement. As education blogger Justin Reich writes, "In the best iPad classrooms, students are constantly making things" (Reich, 2013). That sounds like 10 % tablet, 90 % student.

When learning designers fully use the multisensory functionality of tablet computers, students work through problems, talk aloud to themselves and others, record their work using tablet microphones and cameras, record videos of lab experiments and art project and processes, develop multimedia reports and presentations, facilitate historical reenactments, and engage in all sorts of creative learning. "A big part of what they are doing," says Reich, "is documenting their learning." Reich also comments that such creative learning endeavors "evoke ideas from Project Zero's Making Learning Visible and Visible Thinking programs" (Reich, 2013). Founded at the Harvard Graduate School of Education by philosopher Nelson Goodman in 1967, it is no coincidence that Project Zero was codirected by Howard Gardner (with David Perkins) from 1973 to 2000, the period in which Gardner formulated his theory of multiple intelligences. Readers who want more information about Making Learning Visible should visit the website at http://www.mlvpz.org. The Visible Thinking project also has a website at http://www.visiblethinkingpz.org.

Built-in functions and apps put into students' hands an optimized devise that can facilitate learning in any preferred style or dominant intelligence. Tablets support reading and writing; looking at and creating still and moving images, whether graphic or photographic; hearing live or recorded speech, sounds, and music and recording same; and touching and moving objects or even drawing or painting electronically using the touchscreen. Virtually all of these multisensory functions support and encourage creativity and active construction of knowledge and understanding.

At root, however, is the learning design. Tablets are toolboxes. "Technology does not necessarily improve education," as Gardner and many others have pointed out (Veenema & Gardner, 1996, p. 69). But, as Shirley Veenema and Howard Gardner also say so clearly in their 1996 article, well before the innovation of tablet computing, "If we believe that the mind is neither singular nor revealed in a single language of representation, then our use of technologies should reflect that understanding" (p. 73). That is precisely what the tablet is capable of doing.

15.4 Adaptive Tablet Technology

Tablet computers come equipped with a number of built-in features that allow learning designers to tailor device functionality to meet the needs of students, including those who have serious physical challenges. Three of the five senses—visual, auditory, and kinesthetic, omitting taste and smell—provide a useful way to categorize the principal adaptive features. There are many types of tablets now available, and some share similar functions. The examples in this discussion refer to the most often adopted tablet, Apple's iPad.

Visual. For students with impaired vision, an essential function on the iPad is Speak Selection, which allows the device to read aloud the student's messages, e-mails, e-books, and so on. This function works across applications and can be adjusted in terms of dialect and rate of speech. Voice Dream Reader (http://www.voicedream.com) is an inexpensive iPad app that can provide an enhanced experience: 60 voices, 20 languages, and seamless text navigation.

Another built-in function is VoiceOver, a gesture-based screen reader. Students with impaired vision cannot rely on tactile cues from the smooth glass of the iPad touchscreen, and so VoiceOver provides a spoken description of everything on the screen. Students are told which app they are touching and can find text, images, and other visual elements they may not be able to see.

Siri (on iPad 3 and later) is a built-in personal assistant that uses voice prompts. This function permits students to set reminders, send messages, and look up information. It requires Internet access for at least some functions, however. But it is integrated with VoiceOver.

Dictation (on iPad 3 and later) is a function that converts speech into text for students who cannot see to use the onscreen keyboard. Zoom is a built-in magnifier for students who simply need text and images to appear larger.

Finally, a number of Braille displays and keyboards are available as add-ons to the iPad for visually challenged students. These are wireless devices that link to the tablet using Bluetooth and most integrate with VoiceOver.

Auditory. For students with impaired hearing, a useful function is FaceTime. This video function is standard on iPads with cameras (iPad 2 and later) and allows students to communicate face-to-face with teachers and others across the hall or around the world using a Wi-Fi Internet connection.

Mono Audio is a function that converts stereo to play both audio channels in each ear, which can help students who are deaf or hard of hearing in only one ear. The sound also can be balanced to match hearing differences in a user's ears.

Closed captions are supported on the iPad and available in many education products, such as podcasts and videos. Apple also suggests that GarageBand, available as an iPad app, "can help improve comprehension among deaf and hard of hearing students—particularly those adjusting to new cochlear implants" (see http://www.apple.com/education/special-education/ios/#hearing). Garage Band is a music and voice recording program that comes standard on most Mac computers.

Kinesthetic. Assistive Touch is a built-in function that helps students with limited motor capabilities use the touchscreen effectively. The function reduces the tablet's many gestural commands—such as multiple-finger pinch and swipe gestures—to a simple finger tap. Gestures such as shake and rotate can be made available even if the tablet is firmly mounted to a desk or a wheelchair.

Siri and Dictation, described previously, also are functions that can assist students with motor challenges because they permit voice commands with minimal touch.

The numerous built-in adaptive functions, such as these described for the iPad, should answer most concerns about whether students with sensory physical challenges can participate fully in tablet classrooms. Learning designers also can apply these functions in working with all students to enhance multisensory learning.

15.5 Summary

Options abound in tablet classrooms for learning designers to engage students in multisensory learning. Awareness of multiple intelligences and learning style theories can set a foundation for thinking about how to use tablet functions and apps that go beyond the dominance of the visual to tap auditory and kinesthetic learning options and strategies.

Another frame of reference for learning design is to think of tablet computers as up-sized smartphones, albeit without an actual phone. Smartphone functions are familiar to many students, and so the transition to tablet technology can be virtually seamless. This is increasingly true for even quite young learners and essentially is a given for high-school and college students. Easy familiarity can enhance students' access to learning designs that focus on construction of knowledge and understanding. Echoing Susan Linn, quoted earlier, multisensory functionality helps to ensure that learning designs can be 10 % tablet and 90 % student.

Finally, tablet computers, especially as exemplified by the dominant brand, Apple's iPad, can be adapted to help students with sensory challenges, such as impaired vision, hearing, or motor function. The tablet technology toolbox has tools such students need to engage fully in technology-mediated learning activities. Adaptive functions built into the tablet or added on using apps or after-market devices level the teaching and learning playing field for all students.

References

Gardner, H. (1983). *Frames of mind: The theory of multiple intelligences*. New York: Basic Books.
Gardner, H. (2011) *Multiple intelligences: The first thirty years*. Harvard Graduate School of Education. Retrieved August 7, 2013, from http://howardgardner01.files.wordpress.com
Kolb, D. A. (1984). *Experiential learning: Experience as the source of learning and development*. New Jersey: Prentice-Hall.
Kolb, A. Y., & Kolb, D. A. (2005). Learning styles and learning spaces: Enhancing experiential learning in higher education. *Academy of Management Learning and Education, 4*, 193–212.
Madden, M., Lenhart, A., Duggan, M., Cortesi, S., & Gasser, U. (2013, March 13). *Teens and technology*. Pew Internet. Retrieved August 13, 2013, from http://pewinternet.org/Reports/2013/Teens-and-Tech.aspx

Reich, J. (2013, July 22). The iPad as a tool for creation to strengthen learning. KQED Mind/Shift. Retrieved August 13, 2013, from http://blogs.kqed.org/mindshift/2013/07/potential-and-reality-the-ipad-as-a-tool-for-creation/

Szabo, L. (2011, December 12). Smartest toys for kids can be the simplest. *USA Today*. Retrieved August 13, 2013, from http://usatoday30.usatoday.com/news/health/wellness/story/2011-12-11/Smartest-toys-for-kids-can-be-the-simplest/51816042/1

Veenema, S., & Gardner, H. (1996). Multimedia and multiple intelligences. *The American Prospect, 29*, 69–75.

Walling, D. R. (2006). *Teaching writing to visual, auditory, and kinesthetic learners*. Thousand Oaks, CA: Corwin.

Chapter 16
Can Virtual Be as Effective as Real?

16.1 Introduction

The title of this chapter is a loaded question. There is no doubt that virtual and real are two separate, distinct forms of experience. However, most schools cannot afford to fly their students to Paris to tour the Louvre Museum. So, could a virtual field trip to the Louvre be an effective learning strategy even though it is very different from a real field trip? What about a virtual lab in which students can participate in science experiments to which they would not otherwise have access? What about a game or a simulation?

Most virtual—meaning computer-mediated—learning experiences are conveyed using apps or interactive websites. For the sake of convenience, this chapter is divided into three segments that discuss (1) games and simulations, (2) virtual representations of actual learning activities, and (3) virtual field trips.

The same criteria discussed in previous chapters for choosing e-books, apps, and other media apply to the selection of virtual learning experiences. Virtual experiences that are a good fit for both students and subject matter can ramp up students' construction of new understandings, but virtual programs and activities that are an ill fit can waste time and confuse students. Optimally, learning designs for all subjects can be expanded and enhanced by incorporating appropriate virtual or digitized learning activities using tablet technology.

16.2 A Place for Games and Simulations

High-tech games and simulations seem to provoke controversy, but, in fact, games and let's-pretend activities have long been a standard part of teaching and learning. Now they have merely gone high tech. Spelling bees, math races, and role-playing today can be supplemented using their digital counterparts.

D.R. Walling, *Designing Learning for Tablet Classrooms: Innovations in Instruction*,
DOI 10.1007/978-3-319-02420-2_16, © Springer International Publishing Switzerland 2014

According to Constance Steinkuehler, associate professor of digital media at the University of Wisconsin-Madison and co-director of the Games + Learning + Society (GLS) center there, "Games are architecture for engagement" (MacKay, 2013). Steinkuehler was a participant in February 2013 on a panel at Stanford University that considered games as educational tools. The often-heard criticism that games "dumb down" education was countered by evidence that games can be effective social learning tools. Games can help students develop noncognitive skills, such as patience and discipline, which correlate with success in learning.

Steinkuehler is a former senior policy analyst at the White House Office of Science and Technology. Her GLS group took up the question of boys lagging behind girls in the development of reading skills. Boys often read a grade or two below girls—but they read several grades higher when texts are part of online games. Why? The group's research found that boys who could choose what they read, which the games motivated them to do, pushed themselves to read at higher levels. This result was true for boys struggling as readers and those who already were reading on grade level (MacKay, 2013). Readers who are interested in this issue may also find Penn State professor Ali Carr-Chellman's October 2010 TED Talk on "Gaming to Re-Engage Boys in Learning" worth watching. It can be viewed on the TED website at http://www.ted.com/topics/psychology/page/2.

In today's overly standardized classrooms, seat-time concerns and skill-and-drill in preparation for a mind-numbing array of mandated tests have edged out traditional games. The real purpose of such games—acquisition of noncognitive skills—has been undervalued. Digital Age educational games serve an important purpose and can fill a real gap.

A full review of educational game literature is beyond the scope of this book; however, readers may find a 2012 Pearson research report to be a useful starting point. *A Literature Review of Gaming in Education* examines "claims are that digital games (1) are built on sound learning principles, (2) provide more engagement for the learner, (3) provide personalized learning opportunities, (4) teach twenty-first century skills, and (5) provide an environment for authentic and relevant assessment" (McClarty et al., 2012). Other worthwhile reports include *Moving Learning Games Forward: Obstacles, Opportunities, and Openness* (Klopfer, Osterweil & Salen, 2009) and *Report 8: Literature Review in Games and Learning* (Kirriemuir & McFarlane, 2006).

Simulations are, in many ways, high-tech versions of role-playing. As in role-playing, participating in simulations pushes students to envision themselves in unfamiliar circumstances. An extensive and well-known online platform is Second Life (http://secondlife.com), which provides a gateway to an array of simulations, many of which can be educational. For example, the La Reserva Forest Foundation destination (http://secondlife.com/destination/la-reserva-forest-foundation) can help students learn about forest conservation and regeneration. Other simulations can allow students to take part in historical recreations or play a role in a play, performing with other students on a virtual stage. Newcomers to Second Life will find the orientation video, "Educational Uses of Second Life," helpful. It can be found on YouTube at https://www.youtube.com/watch?v=qOFU9oUF2HA.

In Chap.13, I discussed four critical questions for choosing and using tablet computer apps. Those questions, reframed for games, simulations, and other virtual learning experiences, are equally important here:

- What is the game or simulation intended to do? Does it enhance the learning design?
- How is the game or simulation intended to be used? Does it introduce or reinforce? Will it supplement or substitute for other types of learning activities?
- Is the game or simulation appropriate for the target students? For the learning design?
- Is the game or simulation engaging? Does it allow students to be active learning participants and not merely passive spectators. Recalling the dictum from Chap. 15, is it 10 % game and 90 % student?

Games and simulations are worth discovering and incorporating into learning designs when the answers to these questions are positive. As good as many games and simulations are, however, they should be used judiciously. Oversalting the learning design with virtual experiences runs a risk of marginalizing real, hands-in-the-air, feet-on-the-ground learning activities.

16.3   Virtual Versions of Real-Life Activities

Dissection—frog, fetal pig, and cow's eyeball—used to be a standard activity in high-school biology, but animal treatment issues, material costs, health concerns, and general squeamishness have put the insights that might be gained from hands-on examinations of biological features revealed through dissection out of reach in many schools. Enter virtual dissection. For classrooms that do not have access to preserved frogs or cow's eyeballs and dissection equipment, there are a number of tablet computer apps. One is Frog Dissection from Emantras (http://frogvirtualdissection.com), which is available for a number of platforms: iPad, Mac, Desktop, Intel app, and whiteboard. The tablet apps put this virtual dissection program into the students' hands, but the whiteboard app is a helpful addition for whole-class lecture-discussion.

An Internet search on "virtual dissection" will yield a number of online programs and downloadable apps for a variety of typical dissection activities for various age students. Virtual dissection is impersonal and consequently often can be used with somewhat younger students who are ready for the concepts but not yet ready to use an actual scalpel. The virtual learning apps also make dissection learning activities accessible to students with mental or physical challenges that might otherwise limit their ability to participate.

Virtual explorations also can take learning further for younger students than is possible through real-life activities. For example, there is a Virtual Human Body app (http://www.ikonet.com/en/virtualhumanbody/) for ages 12 and older that general science and biology teachers will find useful to teach students about the inner workings of the human body. The information is as accessible for middle school students as for premed students. The app is available for iPad and Android devices.

Biology is not the only subject in which online programs and apps offer supplements or alternatives to real, hands-on learning activities. The following are a few other examples:

- *Cooking.* How to Cook Everything (http://markbittman.com/app/how-to-cook-everything-cooking-basics/) from Mark Bittman provides cooking basics in app form for iPad. The app might be useful to extend in-class learning or to stimulate independent learning. This is a how-to app, not merely a collection of recipes.
- *Archeology.* Ancient Egypt Virtual 3D Interactive Archaeology Reconstruction: The Raneferef's Hypostyle Hall app from Corinth (http://www.ecorinth.com) lets students explore the architecture of Ancient Egypt. This innovative company also has various other projects, such as apps that let students look inside the International Space Station and micro engines.
- *History.* Museum Box (http://museumbox.e2bn.org) is an online program that allows students to create virtual displays of artifacts found on the Internet. The website poses the question, "What items, for example, would you put in a box to describe your life; the life of a Victorian servant or Roman soldier; or to show that slavery was wrong and unnecessary?" The displays accommodate text, images, sound files, and videos.
- *Music.* Apple's GarageBand (http://www.apple.com/apps/garageband/) is a tablet app that can turn a group of students into a band, using virtual instruments and sophisticated recording tools. Layer instruments, voices, and other effects just like in a real studio. Students can share original compositions and learn about music by using the app alone or while they are learning to play real instruments. Budding composers can ramp up to Notion (http://www.notionmusic.com/products/notionipad.html), an iPad app that functions as a notation editor and playback device.
- *Civics.* In 2009, retired US Supreme Court Justice Sandra Day O'Connor founded iCivics (http://www.icivics.org) to help students and teachers become more knowledgeable about the US democratic system of government. The website offers a wealth of educational video games and other teaching materials, including virtual activities such as drafting an argumentative essay and deciding a court case.

This list is merely illustrative of the vast array of online programs and downloadable apps of virtual activities that can supplement traditional activities. In some circumstances, such virtual learning tools are essential alternatives to real-life activities that may be beyond the mental or physical capabilities of some students or cannot be provided by schools because of budgetary or other constraints.

16.4   Taking a Virtual Field Trip

These days it seems as though most school budgets are strained to the breaking point. The current generation of students probably will not be able to look back on field trips that earlier generations routinely took to supplement in-school learning activities—trips to zoos, factories, forests, museums, power plants, courthouses, well, everywhere. Virtual field trips cannot compare to actual bus trips, but they can be effective as learning tools when there is no bus to be taken. A real bonus is that virtual trips also are not limited to locations within driving distance of the school. Explore a forest on the other side of the globe, stroll through a foreign art museum, and visit a faraway historical site—all are possible on a virtual field trip.

Some websites are set up to facilitate virtual field trips and include guidance for teachers or independent learners. But other websites can be used as virtual field trip destinations with a little forethought in the learning design process. Following is a sampling of just a few possibilities for virtual field trips.

Jefferson Lab (http://www.jlab.org/virtual-tour) offers a virtual field trip that permits students to tour the lab online. (Some features are not enabled for tablet computers but can be accessed in other ways, such as through a laptop and, for whole-class viewing, a whiteboard.) The lab is dedicated to "discovering the fundamental nature of nuclear matter," making this an engaging virtual destination for students studying physics. This is an actual place: the Thomas Jefferson National Accelerator Facility, one of the 17 national laboratories funded by the US Department of Energy. The real-life Jefferson Lab is located in Newport, Virginia. Actual tours of the facilities are limited, especially for visitors under age 18, who are allowed in only during open house, which typically happens only every other year. But the virtual tour is available at any time for students of any age.

One tablet-friendly section is called "Physics Out Loud," which contains videos of scientists explaining common words used in nuclear physics research. These can be accessed from the "Student Zone" section of the website, or students can subscribe to Jefferson Lab's YouTube channel, which features many video programs, including images from the virtual tour.

The Louvre Museum in Paris (http://www.louvre.fr/en/visites-en-ligne) offers virtual tours of this famous art museum. A QuickTime plug-in is required, and so only tablets that support this feature are usable for the tour. However, there are both iPad and Android apps available at minimal prices that will essentially mirror what the website offers for other platforms. Similar style apps are available for virtual tours of London's British Museum, the Hermitage in St. Petersburg, the Uffizi Gallery in Florence, Amsterdam's Rijksmuseum, and the Museum of Modern Art in New York City, among others.

An interesting side benefit of these virtual art museum tours is that many of the museums, especially in other countries, offer tours in the language of the country and, in some cases, other languages. The Musée du Louvre iPad app, for example, is offered in English, French, and Japanese, making these virtual tours useful for language study as well as the study of art, architecture, culture, and history.

Geographic explorations of all sorts can be facilitated by Google Maps and related programs (http://maps.google.com/help/maps/education/learn/index.html). Google Maps lets students be explorers and cartographers to gain knowledge and understanding about geography, map reading, and other geospatial concepts. Among the suggestions for using Google Maps are making collaborative maps, developing a family heritage map, and comparing communities. Google Earth, a related program, offers ways to explore the world through history, science, space science, math, and geography.

Yet another program, Google Street View, provides ways to explore the world's treasures through a variety of collaborations. One such collaboration is the World Wonders Project (http://www.google.com/intl/en/culturalinstitute/worldwonders/), which lets students examine the world through both time and space—the Grand Canyon; the palace of Versailles; the fortified town of Campeche, Mexico; historical villages in Japan; Salamanca, Spain; the Great Barrier Reef; and many other sites. Sites of interest are searchable by location or theme. Each site features maps, descriptive text, photographs, and videos.

Virtual field trips are learning activities that, like real field trips, encourage students to explore their world beyond the classroom walls. These Digital Age excursions can take students farther than any bus. They are well worth incorporating into learning designs for all levels and all types of subject matter.

16.5   Summary

Real and virtual experiences are distinctly different, but the Digital Age allows learning designers to choose which to incorporate into lesson structures. More often than not, it isn't an either-or choice but, rather, a choice of when, why, and how to use both forms of experience. How can a learning design best help learners construct new knowledge and understandings? When should real trump virtual and vice versa? How do learning designers ensure that when virtual activities are used, they are 10 % software and 90 % student?

The choice to use real, hands-on activities usually is superior—but not always. The real has limits—physical, economic, geographic, and so forth. Virtual experiences can sometimes overcome such limitations.

Many digital experiences also are hands-on in different ways, such as navigating a virtual world in a simulation or playing an active software-based game. In some schools, video exercise regimens and full-movement virtual games, such as those available using Nintendo's Wii devices (see http://www.nintendo.com/wii), are being used to supplement traditional physical education or take its place in school facilities without gyms or exercise rooms. Digital Age virtual activities also can be a way to permit students with mental and physical challenges to participate more fully with their non-challenged classmates.

The key to designing learning in tablet classrooms remains the same: Which activities will best allow students to engage in active learning and to construct meaning from their experiences? Real? Virtual? In the Digital Age, the likely answer is both.

References

Kirriemuir, J., & McFarlane, A. (2006). *Report 8: Literature review in games and learning*. Bristol, UK: Futurelab. http://www.futurelab.org.uk

Klopfer, E., Osterweil, S., & Salen K. (2009). *Moving learning games forward: Obstacles, opportunities, and openness*. Education Arcade (M.I.T.). http://education.mit.edu

MacKay, R. F. (2013, March 1) Playing to learn: Panelists at Stanford discussion say using games as an educational tool provides opportunities for deeper learning. *Stanford News*. Retrieved August 21, 2013, from http://news.stanford.edu/news/2013/march/games-education-tool-030113.html

McClarty, K. L., et al. (2012, June) *A literature review of gaming in education*. Pearson. http://www.pearsonassessments.com

Chapter 17
From the Tablet to the Big Picture

17.1 Introduction

Even in highly individualized classrooms, it can be advantageous at times to have all eyes up front—for direct instructions, demonstrations, whole-class activities, student presentations, and other purposes. Supplemental technology can allow teachers and, in some cases, students to put whatever is on their tablet computer onto a larger, classroom screen. This is one form of "big picture," the literal big image on a large screen or whiteboard. Such technology extends the tablet's uses for teaching and learning.

While many schools are issuing tablet computers to their students (iPads dominate the field to date), others are adopting BYOD—for "bring your own device"—strategies, in which tablets feature as one of several potential devices. BYOD means that students are using everything from laptops and tablets to even smaller handheld devices, such as iPods and smartphones. Some key aspects of tablet classrooms versus BYOD classrooms merit discussion.

"Big picture" in the chapter title, however, refers not only to front-of-the-classroom instruction. It also means looking at how learning designers and technology specialists can work toward maximal facilitation of tablet use across multiple classrooms, whether they are next door to each other or on opposite sides of the globe.

The goal for this big-picture chapter, and indeed a current catchphrase, is to work toward "seamless integration." That's really short for "getting everything to work together." This applies to all devices and functions in all sorts of learning situations. It's a big challenge.

D.R. Walling, *Designing Learning for Tablet Classrooms: Innovations in Instruction*,   105
DOI 10.1007/978-3-319-02420-2_17, © Springer International Publishing Switzerland 2014

17.2 Up-Front Instruction

Many classrooms already feature interactive whiteboards (IWBs) that allow computer images to be presented in whole-class scale. IWBs are the computerized cousins of standard whiteboards, which have largely replaced the blackboards and chalk of yesteryear. The interactive element comes in when a finger, a pen, a stylus, or some other object is used to interact with the projected image by means of an electronic interface. For example, an infrared-scan, or IR touch, whiteboard uses scanning software to locate where the instrument is "marking" the whiteboard. These types of IWB can be produced using a variety of surfaces because dry-erase markers and the standard whiteboard are not needed. However, in many cases, this technology is simply used with existing noninteractive whiteboards. Another way to think of IWB technology is that the IR touch feature is essentially external, whereas the touchscreen function of a tablet is internal to the device. But they work in similar ways.

In tablet classrooms, putting the focus up front can be relatively easy. An example of IWB-tablet interface can be illustrated with Apple's ShowMe app (http://www.showme.com). This iPad app allows teachers and students to collaborate and create learning videos, similar in some respects to those available from Khan Academy (see Chap. 13 and http://www.khanacademy.org). Those visuals, which may include sound, can be shared across tablets or downloaded using a Prezi or a Keynote app to project the program on a large scale, such as against a blank wall, a screen, or a whiteboard.

Prezi (http://prezi.com) is a presentation app, which can take on a predesigned ShowMe or can be used to create from scratch a class presentation using images, animation, and sound. The tablet app version of Prezi, however, has some design limitations, which can be overcome by using the version made for laptop or desktop computers. The tablet app is still highly usable.

Keynote (http://www.apple.com/iwork/keynote/) is Apple's tablet version of a PowerPoint. Like Prezi, it will accept a predesigned ShowMe that can be projected for whole-class viewing, or the app can be used to create PowerPoint-style presentations that incorporate images, animations, videos, sound, and so forth.

For learning designers focused on individualizing instruction or developing project-based learning designs, the flexibility exists to use tablets for personalized, hands-on, active learning; for student-student collaborative engagement; and for whole-class as well as one-to-one teacher-student interaction. All of this capacity can be truly liberating for the innovative learning designer. Readers who want to know more about ShowMe might start with the introductory video at http://vimeo.com/38003641. There also is a useful ShowMe blog at http://www.showme.com/blog/.

Another valuable feature of ShowMe is the ability to retain projects for later viewing. This feature allows students to review lessons on their own, during group study time, or at home, where they also can share them with their parents.

17.3 Bring Your Own Device Strategies

Tablet classrooms are proliferating, but some schools are opting to go in a different direction by working to incorporate technology-mediated teaching and learning using the devices students already own. The acronym for this strategy is BYOD, or bring your own device. In many cases, the result is a technologically blended classroom, which can be challenging not only from a technology standpoint but from the perspective of learning design. How does one design learning that "works" with everything from iOS to Android, from laptops to smartphones, and with an assortment of tablets thrown into the mix?

First, educators must acknowledge that the potential for viable BYOD-focused learning design is robust. In June 2013, Project Tomorrow (http://www.tomorrow.org) released its 2012 K-12 student survey findings. The report of the Speak Up National Research Project is titled *From Chalkboards to Tablets: The Emergence of the K-12 Digital Learner* (Project Tomorrow, 2013). Some of the data are telling. For example, 59 % of sixth graders have a personal smartphone; by grade 12, that percentage jumps to 82. Sixty-eight percent of sixth graders have a personal laptop, twelfth graders 73 %. But the figures for personal tablets are perhaps the most revealing of a trend: 53 % of sixth graders have a personal tablet, 48 % of ninth graders, and 40 % of twelfth graders. It would seem that tablet use is growing from the early grades upward. It would not be surprising in a few years to find tablets overtaking laptops among all students, regardless of grade.

Meanwhile, however, these findings illustrate the diverse mix of devices that students might bring to school in a BYOD environment. Add to this complexity the fact that smartphones, laptops, and tablets all come in many varieties from a range of manufacturers, all of whom want to distinguish their devices from their competitors' devices. That's challenging. Fortunately, BYOD is a *potential* technological direction, not an inevitable one. And there are ample reasons why schools might want to shy away from it. A few of these reasons are discussed in the next section.

Second, designing learning for BYOD environments is considerably more complex than designing learning for classrooms with common technology, whether that means 1:1 laptops or tablets. Some challenges include:

- Customizing or individualizing instruction within the limits of a student's available device
- Locating and managing software or apps available (perhaps cloud based) for multiple platforms
- Locating comparable device- or platform-specific apps when multi-platform apps cannot be found
- Using more whole-class instruction or other grouping strategies in order to avoid technology problems, such as lack of compatible apps for different types of devices
- Grouping students according to their available devices, rather than their learning preferences or other characteristics

None of these challenges is insurmountable, but each requires the learning designer to think differently about how best to structure technology-mediated learning activities.

An added consideration, which should not be overlooked, is helping students use their devices effectively. We err in assuming that students are automatically technologically savvy. Granted, many are. However, in tablet classrooms at least some instructional time must be devoted to helping students learn how best to use the designated tablet. In BYOD environments, this device-focused time is multiplied by the number of different devices that students bring with them. That puts pressure on teachers to be familiar with many devices.

17.4 Tablet Classroom Versus BYOD Classroom

This book is about learning design for tablet classrooms and so readers will likely have guessed where my vote will go. In big-picture considerations, cumbersome technological issues may push learning designers to default to less effective and less technology-rich learning designs. While tablets may feature in BYOD environments, the integration of multiple and diverse devices seldom achieves sufficient "seamlessness" to ensure that teaching and learning can be maintained as the real focus of the learning design. With BYOD, the focus can too easily shift to the devices themselves and what they can and cannot do.

American architect Louis Sullivan is credited with coining the mantra of modern, functionalist architecture: "form follows function" (Sullivan, 1896). That is to say, architecture in Sullivan's view—and that of subsequent modernists, such as Frank Lloyd Wright, Walter Gropius, Ludwig Mies van der Rohe, and others—should create structures and spaces based on their intended use or function. In the architecture of learning in technology-mediated environments, it would be wise for educators and education policy makers at all levels to adopt a similar mantra: "device follows design." By this, I mean that learning designs—based on the principles articulated in Chapters 5 through 9—should use tablet (or other) technology to support and enhance teaching and learning, rather than device considerations or limitations, shaping the learning design.

At the same time, the notion of seamless integration should not be confused with standardization. Relatively seamless integration of traditional learning strategies with technologically mediated strategies, even when all students have the same type of device, is a learning design challenge in itself. Most thoughtful educators understand that the idea of all students doing all the same learning activities is counterintuitive as well as counterproductive. That's ultimate standardization and quite opposite from the goals of constructivist teaching and learning, which views students as individuals with distinct needs, interests, abilities, and aspirations.

In an Australian BYOD report, Joseph Sweeney comments piquantly, "Standarisation should not be viewed as a goal in itself. In the age of consumerisation, standardisation is increasingly around software and cloud services, with the choice of device being of little relevance" (Sweeney, 2012, p. 20). But Sweeney acknowledges, "As the number of different devices and software environments increases, so too does complexity….[T]he more control teachers need over the learning environment, the more standardisation benefits the learning environment" (p. 20).

Another perspective is offered by *Bring Your Own Device to School* (Dixon and Tierney, no date, 2012?), underwritten by Microsoft. This white paper discusses various BYOD deployment models and includes a pros-and-cons section.

It's a tricky balancing act. Optimal learning is likely to result when standardization, seamless integration, and individualization are in balance. At this time, such balance seems more likely to be achieved in tablet classrooms than in BYOD classrooms.

17.5 A Global Big Picture

Another aspect of the big picture in learning design is collaborative learning, not merely among students in the same classroom but between classrooms. The collaborating classrooms might be within the same school building, across town, or in different parts of the world. Learning designers can capitalize on tablet technology to structure learning projects that involve students in both synchronous and asynchronous collaborative activities.

For example, Google Drive (http://www.google.com/drive/about.html?authuser=0) is a free tablet app that is available for iOS and Android devices. The app allows students to share information, such as documents and spreadsheets, and to chat in real time (synchronous). They can collaboratively write and edit and then share what they have done with their teachers and other students. The documents also can be stored and shared asynchronously, and in some cases, projects can be worked on without a network connection and shared later when Internet connectivity is available.

Another example is Groupboard (http://www.groupboard.com/products/), a free online whiteboard and chat app. This app also is available for iPad and Android tablets. The free version allows a limited number of users; however, paid versions allow many more. Related apps include a more advanced Groupboard Designer, similar to Groupboard but with more features, and Groupworld, which provides customizable web-conferencing. Groupboard Designer and Groupworld also are available as iPad and Android tablet apps.

Web-conferencing software allows learning designers to structure collaborative learning projects and activities that connect students who may by physically widely separated. File sharing is merely a starting point. Video and audio components truly personalize interactions, and it's important for students to see and hear one another.

A number of real-time communication apps can provide for face-to-face interaction, sometimes with or without other web-conferencing components, such as desktop sharing and whiteboards. Skype (http://www.skype.com) is among the most well known, and the app works on a variety of tablet devices: Windows 8, iPad, Kindle Fire, and Android tablets. The app supports audio calling, messaging, video communication, and file sharing.

All of these technological tools can help learning designers create opportunities for global connectedness. Kristen Wideen, a primary school teacher in Windsor, Ontario, Canada, writes a blog about teaching and learning in her grade 1/2 classroom and describes her work in Mrs. Wideen's Blog (http://www.mrswideen.com). On April 14, 2013, she uploaded a post titled "How My Learning Environment Has Evolved," in which she described her approach as a "classroom with no walls." She wrote, "Video conferencing, blogging, creating videos and books, teaching and learning from other peers in the classroom, in the school and in the world about what they are interested in is embedded into the daily instruction of my classroom" (Wideen, 2013). Wideen's students in Canada regularly communicate with their counterparts in a couple of schools in Singapore by tweeting, using Skype, or other means.

Learning designers and other educators also need to connect with colleagues both near and far. Connected Educators (http://connectededucators.org) is one organization specifically dedicated to that purpose. The organization was envisioned in the US 2010 National Educational Technology Plan. (For an explanation of this plan, readers may wish to consult a chapter I cowrote with Phillip Harris about policies governing education technology practice and research; see Harris & Walling, 2014.) Connected Educators is a project of the Office of Educational Technology at the US Department of Education and provides a wealth of information for educators. This effort also includes ConnectED, which the White House describes as an initiative that will "within 5 years, connect 99 % of America's students to the digital age through next-generation broadband and high-speed wireless in their schools and libraries" (see http://www.whitehouse.gov/blog/2013/06/06/what-connected).

Global connectedness for collaborative learning and collegial sharing represent another perspective on the big picture of how tablet computers can change—indeed, are already transforming—teaching and learning at all levels.

17.6   Summary

The idea of a "big picture" can be taken in many directions. Literally, making whatever is on the tablet computer big by putting it up front on a screen or an IWB is one direction. Tablet technology can facilitate learning designs that need the focus up front in the classroom, whether it is for sharing student projects or providing direct instruction.

When tablets are among the many devices in BYOD classrooms, they do not lose their unique attributes. But learning designers in BYOD environments face many challenges—both technological and logistical—to coordinate technology-mediated learning. Those challenges can be daunting. At best, BYOD runs the risk of learning designers needing to focus more on devices than designs, just the opposite of the focus needed for optimal teaching and learning. At worst, the challenges presented by multiple types of devices can discourage learning designers from using some forms of technology that might otherwise ramp up students' learning opportunities and options.

Finally, using tablet technology to foster broader learning connections among students not only within the same classroom or school but also in widely separated— sometimes globally separated—classrooms is another interpretation of "big picture." Many students learn most effectively in community, and creating communities of learners can be a globally expanded concept when learning designers tap the collaborative technological power of tablet computers. Such collaboration and communication also benefits educators when they can connect with widely separated colleagues.

References

Dixon, B., & Tierney S. (2012). *Bring your own device to school.* Microsoft (Windows in the Classroom), no date? http://www.microsoft.com/education

Harris, P., & Walling, D. R. (2014). Policies governing educational technology practice and research (Chapter 50). In J. M. Spector et al. (Eds.), *Handbook of research on educational communication and technology* (4th ed., pp. 627–640). New York: Springer.

Project Tomorrow. (2013). *From chalkboards to tablets: The emergence of the K-12 digital learner.* Speak Up National Research Project annual poll for 2012). Irvine, CA: Author. http://www.tomorrow.org

Sullivan, L. H. (1896, April). The tall office building artistically considered. *Lippincott's Magazine.* http://archive.org

Sweeney, J. (2012). *BYOD in education: A report for Australia and New Zealand.* Intelligent Business Research Services Ltd. (Australia). http://i.dell.com

Wideen, K. (2013, April 14). How my learning environment has evolved. *Mrs. Wideen's Blog.* Retrieved September 20, 2013, from http://www.mrswideen.com/2013/04/how-my-learning-environment-has-evolved.html

Chapter 18
Tablet Take-Home Strategies

18.1 Introduction

The portability of tablet computers makes them ideal for take-home learning strategies, from flipped classroom assignments to extended practice or independent learning. Tablet-based learning at home also can be a means of increasing parents' involvement in their children's education. The major issues affecting take-home strategies involve access to tablet devices and Internet connectivity. These issues will influence potential learning designs.

Several accessibility models exist for tablet learning, ranging from full 1:1 (one-to-one) tablet access both at school and at home to shared, or restricted, tablet access only at school. In situations that do not permit students to take school-issued tablets home, students may be able to access tablet-based or technology-mediated learning activities in other ways. However, the economic question of technology haves and have-nots cannot be ignored if learning designers want to create optimal learning circumstances.

Connectivity also is a consideration in take-home learning strategies. Fortunately, much of what can be done on a tablet does not require Internet connectivity. Tablets can function as independent—freestanding—portable learning laboratories and libraries. Self-contained apps, recorded audiovisual content, and saved documents all facilitate the extension of learning to the home and other nonschool settings.

18.2 Accessibility Issues

Several tablet classroom models exist, and learning designers must work within each model's constraints to create optimal teaching and learning situations. Following are four models, each with pros and cons that learning designers need to consider.

D.R. Walling, *Designing Learning for Tablet Classrooms: Innovations in Instruction*, DOI 10.1007/978-3-319-02420-2_18, © Springer International Publishing Switzerland 2014

Full 1:1 accessibility. The optimal model for student learning in a tablet environment treats tablet computers essentially like textbooks. They are issued or rented to students on an individual basis, and students use them in school, at home, or in other places. Tablet computers are intended to be personal learning devices, and so 1:1 individualized usage allows each student to engage fully with the device, exploring not only those features that are used in lessons but also other features that can contribute to independent learning. Students can take their tablets home, just like their textbooks, to pursue independent practice or to prepare for future in-school lessons (à la a flipped classroom, see Chap. 13). The downside to allowing students to take home their school-provided tablets includes increased potential for damage or loss—and, of course, forgetting to bring it to school. Most districts have usage policies, insurance, and other mechanisms to help mitigate these potential problems.

In-school 1:1 accessibility. Some schools issue tablets to students on an individual basis for use throughout the school day but require students to leave their devices at school. This model allows students to become familiar with device features related to lessons and school assignments but does little to encourage independent learning unless that is specifically built into the learning design during the school day. As more textbooks become available to schools as eTextbooks, students who cannot take home their tablets also will not have access to their textbooks, which can limit independent learning and practice. Some schools are somewhat flexible, allowing students to check out their tablets for home use under certain conditions.

Shared accessibility. In some situations, a set of tablets is maintained in the classroom for students to use only when they are in that classroom. The tablets usually are used by multiple students, there may not even be one tablet per student in a given class, and tablets and laptops may be mixed. "In grades one, two, and three, you're probably fine with that," according to technology consultant Sam Gliksman (quoted in Schaffhauser, 2013). Gliksman operates iPads for Education (http://ipadeducators.ning.com), a Ning network. He believes that from grade four onward, however, students' need for personal space argues for 1:1 tablets. With shared accessibility, only some of the advantages of tablet technology can be realized. Learning designers may have a limited range of options for compatible software for large-group learning, which may proactively encourage individualized instruction. Yet, for many learning designs, the negatives will outweigh the positives for effective technology-mediated teaching and learning. Shared accessibility rarely supports tablet take-home strategies because most schools with limited tablets do not check them out to students for at-home use except in extraordinary circumstances (such as special needs or extended illness).

BYOD accessibility. Tablets may figure in the mix of devices that students bring to school in bring-your-own-device situations. While 1:1 computers are standard in BYOD classrooms, little else is standardized. Therein lies the challenge for learning designers. In some cases, learning designs will need to be customized for individual students or groups of students with compatible devices, both for in-class technology-mediated teaching and learning and for take-home learning strategies. (See a more extended discussion of BYOD in Chap. 17.)

These configurations represent the four main types of tablet classrooms. Each offers opportunities and challenges in the development of effective designs for learning outside the school setting.

18.3   Haves and Have-Nots

One cannot ignore, though some politicians and policy makers try, the socioeconomic realities that affect teaching and learning. According to researcher Sean F. Reardon (2013), "The black-and-white achievement gap was considerably larger than the income achievement gap among cohorts born in the 1950s and 1960s, but now it is considerably smaller than the income achievement gap"—that is, the difference between achievement of students from low- and high-income families (p. 11). Reardon is among a number of researchers who have concluded that income inequality in the United States over the past 30–40 years has increased dramatically. He also believes that schools can play an important role in mitigating the negative effects of the income gap. One aspect of that role is to ensure that students have access to resources, including technology. This is one of the strongest arguments for 1:1 tablet classrooms.

Interestingly, except for the extremely poor and in isolated cases, many children even in impoverished homes have access to computer technology in some form. Smartphones, in particular, are becoming nearly universal, and they are a close parallel of tablet technology in many ways. According to one 2013 study, by the time students enter high school, 51 % are carrying a smartphone; nearly a quarter of all K-12 students are doing so (Grunewald 2013). This study also found that 78 % of families own a portable computer. The family computer is used daily by 51 % of the children (ages 3–18) in the family. Smart phones came next, with 77 % of families owning one (or more) and 65 % of children in those families using them. Tablet computers ranked above the iPod Touch and e-readers, being owned by 46 % of families, with 47 % of children in those families using a tablet daily. These figures tend to support alternative learning options for students in situations where schools cannot provide full 1:1 accessibility to tablets.

A possible upside to limited access can be sharing devices in the home, which also can offer opportunities for students and their parents to share what is going on in school. Creative learning designers can foster this parent-child communication by giving consideration to side-by-side learning activities, such as shared reading in the early grades.

18.4   Connectivity Issues

Many computer features, regardless whether they are on tablets or other devices, require Internet access. Online downloads are the most common way that new software applications, or apps, are obtained. Once installed, many apps rely on wireless Internet connectivity to function, such as to stream media (audio, video) or to connect to cloud services. When learning designers develop activities to engage students at home, they must consider whether students have Wi-Fi access at home. In some situations this may be the case, but in most communities home Wi-Fi will not be universal. Consequently, it is a good idea to consider take-home strategies that do not depend on Internet connectivity.

For example, most e-books and eTextbooks, once downloaded, reside on the tablet device and can be read without an Internet connection. However, some features built into e-books, such as links or streaming media, may not be available unless the device is online.

Note-taking programs, such as Evernote (http://evernote.com), and programs that allow file sharing across devices, such as Dropbox (http://www.dropbox.com), can be used on a tablet device without being connected to the Internet. The information added in such programs simply will sync (usually automatically) with other linked devices the next time the device is online.

Students who write reports and other types of text online using word-processing apps, such as Apple's Pages (http://www.apple.com/apps/iwork/pages/) or Google Docs (http://www.google.com/mobile/drive/) for Android devices, can use the program regardless of connectivity and upload resulting documents to a cloud server or other sharing or storage option whenever they next have connectivity. Pages is part of Apple's iWorks suite of apps, and Google Docs is part of Google Drive, a similar suite of apps. Both suites include spreadsheet and presentation apps, as well as word processing.

In similar fashion, a number of freestanding learning apps do not depend on Internet connectivity after the initial download. An example is Hands-On Equations (http://www.borenson.com), which uses imbedded video introductions and interactive kinesthetics to engage learners in the basics of algebra. The app functions offline, but, of course, any update downloads will need Internet connectivity.

18.5 Work Anywhere

Accessibility and connectivity are tough issues for students who cannot take their tablet home, do not have an alternative device to use at home, or if they have a device do not have an Internet connection at home. Some solutions are possible; however, they mainly apply to older students when they involve non-supervised settings.

In-school facilities. Study areas, computer labs, and libraries in some schools can offer spaces and devices, with Internet connectivity, that students can use outside regular class time. Such spaces are normally supervised and so can be helpful for students of all ages. In some communities, such facilities are open to the general public as well, usually after normal school hours.

Public libraries and community centers. Many public libraries offer patrons free Wi-Fi, and a growing number are able to provide public access devices. Most of the commonly available devices are desktop computers, but some libraries are exploring other device accessibility, including tablets. For example, in the spring of 2012, five public libraries in northeastern Kansas installed iPad labs, the first of their kind in that area (Alexander, 2012).

Similarly, community centers in some localities are offering public space with Wi-Fi access for both adults and children to use. Some libraries and community centers encourage parents and students to work together, particularly in the case of younger children.

Commercial establishments. Bookstores, coffee shops, fast-food restaurants, and a number of other commercial enterprises offer free Wi-Fi to patrons. Anyone who lives in a college town can bear witness to the numbers of students who routinely "camp out" in local cafés, using free Wi-Fi to work on class assignments. While these settings have many limitations and cannot be used by younger students, high schoolers often can fit in with their only slightly older undergrad peers.

Alternative devices. Some alternative devices, such as smartphones, come with built-in Wi-Fi and tablet-like capabilities. Some take-home work can be done on these devices and then transferred to a tablet. A visiting German high-school student we hosted one school year routinely did written homework assignments on his iPod Touch and then transferred them to his school-based tablet or home-based laptop. Often, if we were driving across town, he would be doing his homework while sitting in the passenger seat.

For dedicated learning designers and engaged students, the old saw about "where there's a will, there's a way" turns out to be true.

18.6 Summary

There is no general consensus on whether homework is necessary or even desirable. Noted education author Alfie Kohn (2006) points out in his book, *The Homework Myth,* that no study has ever found a correlation between homework and academic achievement. Many educators and parents view homework as an unnecessary "second shift" imposed on students.

When working at home is seen as necessary or desirable, then learning designers can consider a number of tablet take-home strategies. What will work in any given situation, however, will depend on accessibility and connectivity. When students have full 1:1 access to tablet computers that they can use both in and out of school, then accessibility is not an issue. A lower level of accessibility will require greater creativity from both learning designers and students.

Similarly, full device access in homes with Wi-Fi connectivity makes linking to the Internet a nonissue. But if connectivity is not available in the home, then tablet take-home strategies need to be modified to concentrate activity around apps that are freestanding.

The combinations of accessibility and connectivity are seemingly infinite. They will differ from school to school and, often, from classroom to classroom within a single school. Creative learning designs, however, will allow teachers and students (and sometimes parents and other community members) to approach teaching and learning using strategies that match the needs of students.

References

Alexander, D. (2012). Public library iPad labs. *Northeast Kansas Library System*. Retrieved September 26, 2013, from http://www.nekls.org/nekls-services/econtent/devices-services/ios/miami-county-library-ipad-labs/

Grunewald Associates LLC. (2013). *Living and learning with mobile devices: What parents think about mobile devices for early childhood and K-12 learning*. Bethesda, MD: Author. http://www.grunwald.com

Kohn, A. (2006). *The homework myth: Why our kids get too much of a bad thing*. Boston: Da Capo.

Reardon, S. F. (2013). The widening income achievement gap. *Educational Leadership, 70*, 10–16.

Schaffhauser, D. (2013, April 10). 7 Tips for effectively managing your iPad classroom. *THE Journal*. Retrieved September 25, 2013, from http://thejournal.com/articles/2013/04/10/7-tips-for-managing-your-ipad-classroom.aspx

Chapter 19
Do You Moodle?

19.1 Introduction

The more computerized the classroom, the greater the need for digital management tools. Just as there are programs and apps for teaching and learning, there also are tablet-friendly tools that teachers can use to manage everything from documents and photos to attendance and grades.

The title of this chapter refers to Moodle (http://moodle.org/), perhaps the most widely used open source course management system (CMS). Moodle is short for Modular Object-Oriented Dynamic Learning Environment. Course management systems also are referred to as learning management systems (LMS) or virtual learning environments (VLE). Moodle provides options for deploying full-scale online courses or supplementing face-to-face instruction. The latter means that Moodle can support scheduling, lesson planning, grade reporting, and so forth.

As an open source platform, Moodle also allows other developers to create programs that interface with Moodle, which exponentially broadens the base of available programs. Based in Australia, Moodle boasts more than 70,000 registered sites with more than 50 million users in more than 200 countries. The numbers keep growing, and conferences of users—called MoodleMoots—are scheduled at various times literally around the world. Check the Moodle website for schedules. For a primer on using Moodle, there is *Using Moodle* (second edition, 2007) by Jason Cole and Helen Foster. Updated information also is available in *Moodle News* (http://www.moodlenews.com), an e-newsletter website.

19.2   How Course Management Systems Work

In Moodle schools, teachers can benefit from downloading the official Moodle iPad app, called My Moodle (http://docs.moodle.org/22/en/My_Moodle), which is designed to work with the regular Moodle website but cannot be used independently. Moodbile (http://www.moodbile.org/) for Android has similar features.

Moodle is not without competitors on the commercial side of the marketplace. One is Skyward (http://www.skyward.com/), which offers a student management suite that integrates scheduling, grading, lesson planning, textbook tracking, and many other elements of K-12 school management. Skyward Mobile Access is an iPad app for students, parents, and school staff who use Skyward Family Access, Student Access, or Employee Access—all part of the total package. A comparable Android app was in development as this chapter was written.

For educators in schools not hooked into a schoolwide CMS/LMS/VLE, there are many other apps that can be used to help manage teaching and learning. The iPad apps are available from the App Store. Prices for most vary from free to about $10. Many also are available for Android, BlackBerry, and other platforms. Browse the Android App Store (http://www.android.com/apps/) and BlackBerry App World (http://appworld.blackberry.com/).

Among the most useful apps are those that help organize "stuff"—documents, photos, videos, and so forth. These organizers use cloud computing that, simply defined, allows a user to access files stored centrally on a trusted server. This server can then be accessed through any available device, such as the user's smartphone, tablet, laptop, or desktop—or all of these. Sam Johnston's logical diagram, Figure 19.1, offers a helpful way to think about cloud computing.

Teachers in tablet classrooms invariably have one or more other computers in addition to a tablet. No one wants to be searching every device to find *that* file, that half-remembered something-or-other that is really needed *right now.* Or, for that matter, why try to remember to put important dates on all of your calendars or to find those important ideas you jotted down somewhere for a new lesson? This is the moment when some form of synchronous, readily accessible storage is essential. A cloud computing service is the answer.

For Apple users, the cloud service that comes built in on the iPad and newer Mac computers is iCloud (http://www.icloud.com/), launched in 2011. Like other cloud services, iCloud allows users to back up files of all sorts and then get to them from any of their iOS (Apple's Unix-like operating system for iPod, iPhone, and iPad) devices or Mac computers using a Lion (OS X, 10.7 version) or later operating system. Users can set cloud preferences to sync all or only some features automatically. For example, it might be helpful to have all calendars and contacts synced but not photos.

Not working in an Apple environment? Or just want something different from iCloud? Dropbox (https://www.dropbox.com/) is another such tool. This app lets users save photos, documents, and videos so that they are available on all of their computers. It works with Windows, Mac, Linux, iPad, iPhone, Android, and BlackBerry.

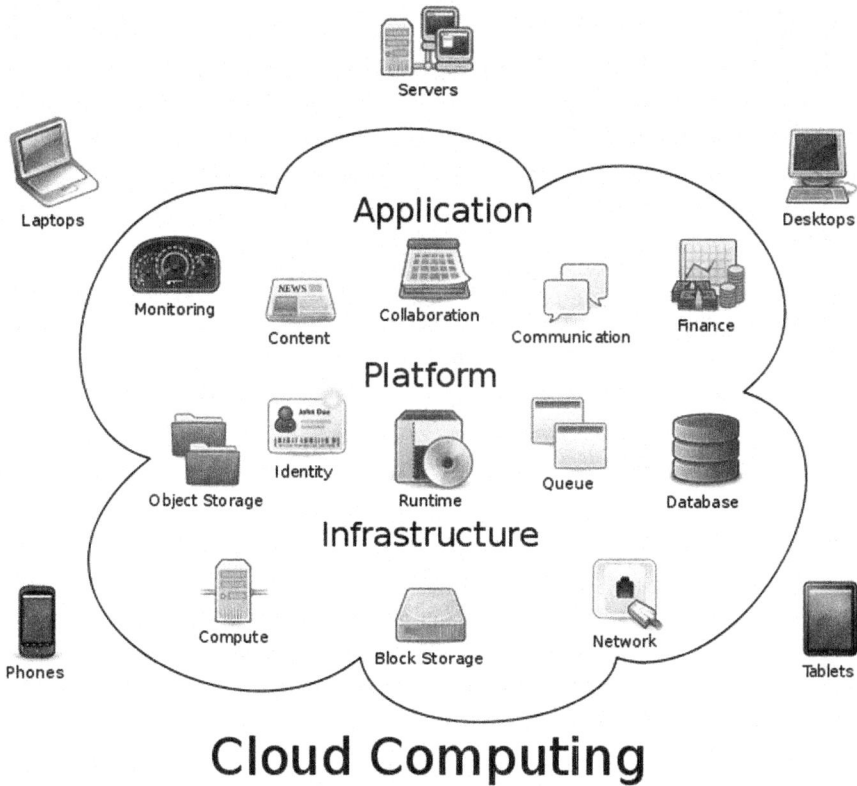

Fig. 19.1 Cloud computing (courtesy of Wikimedia Commons)

Dropbox is (at least for the time being) the leading cloud computing service. But quite a few other services are coming online.

Technophiles had been waiting in great anticipation for the giant Google to enter the cloud computing field, which it did in April 2012 with Google Drive (https:// drive.google.com/), downplaying the new service as merely an expansion of the company's Docs service. At launch, much of this cloud computing system was still being developed, such as apps for iOS devices. However, regular expansions and updates—not only by Google but also by other developers—ensure that if an app is not available at any given moment, then in all likelihood it soon will be.

A recent expansion, for instance, has been Google Hangouts, which extends the Google Drive suite by using a social network component to connect teachers and students in various ways. A teacher can broadcast a presentation (by a teacher, a guest expert, or a student), archive the broadcast, and share it with colleagues or students. Google Hangouts can let educators present at distance conferences that they cannot attend in person. For more information, readers might check out Andrew Marcinek's 2013 blog post on Edutopia (see Refs.).

A couple of other cloud services worth mentioning are Microsoft's SkyDrive (http://skydrive.live.com/) and SugarSync (https://www.sugarsync.com/). Both work with a variety of devices, though SkyDrive with fewer than SugarSync as of this writing.

The myriad of apps available for management, like those for other purposes, reinforces a useful mantra: I choose and use. Learning designers need to pick those apps that provide the maximum functionality that suits their work, study, and instructional styles and ignore, delete, or deselect the rest.

Following is a concise selection of apps for specific purposes. They are grouped in three key categories: note-taking (for teachers, not students), professional reading, and attendance and grading.

19.3   Note-Taking

The portability of tablet computers and other handheld devices at most teachers' disposal argues for note-taking functionality. Teachers need to make notes about new ideas and lessons, observations of students, miscellaneous reminders, and so forth. Notes made on one device need to sync automatically across devices so that they are available in class, at home, or on the go. Evernote (http://evernote.com/) is one of the most functional of many note-taking apps and works across most platforms. Users can capture virtually everything they see or hear, from articles to photos and video clips, make notes, and save everything to be available on all of a user's devices.

Springpad (http://springpad.com/) for iOS and Android, like Evernote and several others, allows users to clip articles from the Web or include photos. Users organize and share "notebooks." OneNote (http://office.microsoft.com/en-us/onenote/) originated as a component of Microsoft Office. It may seem complicated to novice users but has a number of useful functions that complement Microsoft's Office software suite. Simplenote (http://simplenoteapp.com/) is another app. At launch, it was aimed primarily at the iOS market but it has expanded. Several forms of client software will interface with Simplenote.

All of the above note-taking apps are free in their basic form and come with premium services for a price.

A word about digital handwriting is necessary. For many users of the iPad and other tablets, typing notes is a nuisance. (Typing on tablet computers with virtual keyboards is a nuisance in any case for those of us who are used to touch-typing and need to feel the keys.) Handwriting notes on the iPad screen can be a convenient time-saver. Penultimate (http://www.cocoabox.com/) allows users to handwrite or draw on the screen using a soft-point stylus or fingertip. In 2012, Evernote bought Cocoa Box, the Penultimate developer, so it makes sense that the digital handwriting app syncs with Evernote. It also syncs with Dropbox, and Penultimate notes can be emailed, too.

Another sort of annotation involves highlighting or drawing on images, such as maps and photos. Skitch (http://evernote.com/skitch/), also recently acquired by

Evernote, lets users circle elements, add arrows for emphasis, and otherwise label and annotate a captured image. The annotated image can be emailed, filed, or shared.

Converting handwriting to text is another matter. Optical character recognition (OCR) software that will reliably recognize handwriting is still in its infancy. Users who scribble notes in Penultimate and then move them to Evernote can use a search function that sometimes will find the handwritten word, but it's a hit-or-miss proposition.

MyScript Memo (http://www.visionobjects.com/) is an iOS app that converts handwriting to digital text that can then be emailed or stored. The download is essentially a free trial, then users pay an in-app fee to do anything with the resulting text. The app is suitable only for short notes. MyScript Notes Mobile is this app's big brother—more features, higher price. Both apps incorporate some 30 recognition languages, which could be a plus in some circumstances.

19.4   Professional Reading

The pace at which new professional information arrives on teachers' digital devices—e-mails, e-blasts and e-newsletters, RSS feeds, and so on—is mind-boggling. Robust reader apps can help users make the most of the information they want to read and remember, but they may need several apps to touch all the bases.

GoodReader for iPad (http://www.goodiware.com/) is a PDF reader that allows users to annotate what they read, manage (copy, move, rename, organize) files, and transfer them using Dropbox, SugarSync, and other cloud services. Similar apps are available for Android. Incidentally, Good.iWare, the GoodReader producer, also makes a comparable calculator app called GoodCalculator, though at this writing it was available only for iPhone and iPod, not iPad.

Bluefire Reader (http://www.bluefirereader.com/) is for e-books and PDF content with available bookmarks, annotations, and highlights. It works with iOS and Android. All that and more once could be found in Google Reader, which was one of the most popular and versatile of the reader apps when I began writing this book. It has now been discontinued, which provides a good example of the ever-changing nature of technology and related software.

As for sources of reading material, the options are limitless. Apple's iBooks (http://www.apple.com/ipad/built-in-apps/) is one of the most electronically elegant e-readers around. Among other things, users can shop for books (both free and paid, delivered through iTunes), organize bookshelves by topic or author, add PDFs, and sync everything across devices. Search features help find words and phrases quickly, and users can takes notes as they read and then organize them, highlight text, and look up unfamiliar words in the dictionary. The text display is crisp and can be customized in terms of color, size, and brightness. A VoiceOver function will allow the iPad to read a book aloud.

If the 700,000 titles available in the iBooks store are not enough, then there are always other e-book suppliers, such as the giant online bookseller Amazon (http://www.amazon.com/). Amazon's Kindle app is a free download for various types of tablet computers. Although Kindle is not as visually elegant as iBooks, it has many of the same functions. Amazon's range of education-related e-books is vast.

Sony Reader (http://ebookstore.sony.com/download/) and Barnes and Noble's Nook e-book reader (http://www.barnesandnoble.com/NOOK) are the other big names among e-readers. Both are available as apps for tablets of various kinds. They share many features with iBooks and Kindle. Like the stores associated with the others, these two also offer access to an array of titles.

Readers looking for a source that concentrates on e-books and has a large section devoted to education-related titles should check out eBooks.com (http://www.ebooks.com/), which has titles for Apple and Android devices and a variety of e-readers, including those mentioned above and others.

The advantages of e-books are numerous. Download as many titles as you like and your backpack or briefcase is not going to get any heavier. Most e-books do not cost as much as their traditional paper counterparts. You can take all the notes you want, organize them, and never lose them. Start reading on one device and continue on another using cloud sync functionality. On the downside, not every title is available for every e-reader and so users may need to download several reading apps. And, of course, some books are not available in electronic form at all.

19.5 Attendance and Grading

Two routine but essential elements of any teacher's workload are taking attendance and recording grades. There are several apps for iPads and other tablet computers to make these two chores faster and easier. One of these is TeacherKit, a free, simple, intuitive iPad app (check iTunes) that lets teachers track attendance, grades, and behavior of students. TeacherKit has a Facebook page at https://www.facebook.com/teacherkitapp. Users who need a more sophisticated iPad app (which is not free) can turn to TeacherTool (http://www.teachertool.de/cms/). This app was developed in Germany by Udo Hilwerling and has earned top awards in Germany and Switzerland. A simpler, free (and not as highly rated) version also is available, called TeacherTool One, which can be found in iTunes.

GradeBook Pro (http://gradebookapp.com/) is an iPad app that offers an extensive suite of features, from managing attendance and recording grades to keeping notes on individual student assignments and generating PDF reports of various kinds. Content can be shared, emailed, or added to Dropbox. The same company (Eric Lombardo) also produces Grade, a student-oriented iPad/iPhone/iPod app so that students can keep track of their grades in various classes.

Android for Academics (http://androidforacademics.com/) produces several apps, including Grade Book for Professors and Attendance. Both of these apps sync using Google Spreadsheets so that teachers can maintain their attendance and grades across devices. This developer also offers Grade Rubric for teachers who use grading rubrics, Grade Ticker for point scoring, and Grade Chart for basic item analysis.

Not all attendance and grading apps are generic. Some subject-specific apps are worth reviewing. For example, if writing is a focus of instruction, then learning designers might want to check into the apps from Gatsby's Light Publications (http://gatsbyslight.com/), which include Essay Grader, an iPad app that allows for extensive feedback on students' writing. This company also produces apps for students studying literary analysis and essay writing.

19.6 Summary

A single chapter devoted to management apps can only scratch the surface. To explore more apps available in the digital universe that someone has tried and recommended, readers should try Internet searches using various keywords, such as "attendance and grading apps" or "note-taking apps." The result will be websites galore, including nonprofit organizations, commercial producers, and individuals who write informative blogs, such as Jeff Piontek's Apps in Education (http://appsineducation.blogspot.com/).

Also, don't forget the wikis, such as Ipadschools, which has a page devoted to teacher tools apps (http://ipadschools.wikispaces.com/Teacher+Tools+Apps).

Learning designers who want to get the most out of tablet-mediated teaching and learning will want to devote significant attention to how effective learning management can be designed for tablet classrooms. The options are sufficiently varied to suit virtually any learning situation.

References

Cole, J., & Foster, H. (2007). *Using moodle* (2nd ed.). Sebastopol, CA: O'Reilly Media.
Marcinek, A. (2013, March 19). Google hangouts as Edtech: Connecting sharing, and learning. *Edutopia*. Retrieved September 30, 2013, from http://www.edutopia.org/blog/google-hangouts-connecting-sharing-learning-andrew-marcinek

Chapter 20
Tackling Trouble in the Tablet Classroom

20.1 Introduction

This chapter examines how learning designers and teachers at all levels in tablet classrooms can approach some key Digital Age challenges that can spell trouble. The challenges are widely varied and not inconsiderable. But a few important ones are worth addressing in this final chapter. Overcoming these challenges will permit learning designers to create optimal conditions for teaching and learning.

The clearest path may be to consider these challenges from the systemic to the specific. Systemic challenges tend to involve school (usually district) infrastructure and are least amenable to direct solution by learning designers. However, those responsible for designing and delivering learning opportunities can articulate technology-related educational needs that must be addressed through policies and procedures at the system level and thereby influence policy outcomes.

More specific trouble spots can be parsed in general into devices and their use. Device challenges center on the tablet and its software—how they work (or don't work). In this arena, learning designers and other practitioners need to learn both how to prevent device issues from arising and how to address them when they occur. In earlier chapters, I suggested that a tablet computer is a toolbox. Sometimes the box (the tablet device) itself needs fixing, and sometimes problems surface that involve specific tools (software and apps).

Usage challenges offer a third arena that must concern learning designers. In any computer-mediated learning environment, whether the computers are desktops, laptops, or tablets, there is potential for abuse and misuse. Consequently, this portion of the discussion will focus on commonly troublesome use issues, such as plagiarism.

Knowing the types of trouble that might arise and having a proactive plan for addressing problems can help learning designers avoid or solve problems that get in the way of effective teaching and learning.

D.R. Walling, *Designing Learning for Tablet Classrooms: Innovations in Instruction*, 127
DOI 10.1007/978-3-319-02420-2_20, © Springer International Publishing Switzerland 2014

20.2   Systemic Challenges

Issues that arise at the school or district level tend to involve either policy or capacity, sometimes both. Policy issues range broadly, but many touch on matters of security—security of devices, security of personal information, security of the network, and so forth. For example, as devices proliferate and include not only school-issued computers but also personal devices brought to school by educators and students alike, school district concerns often arise over network security. In a "flat" network, all users have the same level of access. This sounds equitable, but it can leave the network vulnerable to misuse. Consequently, many districts are moving to a "user-authentication" network, in which different types of users are granted differentiated levels of access. A log-in system also can be set to give users time limits for access. For example, a principal's log-in might last a week, a teacher's a day, and a student's a class period (Roscoria, 2011).

Access, or connectivity, issues also can surface when schools use filtering to block or attempt to block certain portions of the Internet, usually as a way to limit students' access to potentially dangerous or unsavory websites (see also Chap. 5). From a technological standpoint, such policies tend to be problematic. Students who are determined to find a way around such filters usually can. Recall the example in Chap. 2 about the MIT experiment in which a group of elementary-age Ethiopian students taught themselves using Motorola Xoom tablets, having never been exposed to computer technology beforehand. One of the children, an 8-year-old, went so far as to figure out how to turn on the device camera, which had been disabled to conserve memory space (Associated Press, 2013a). High school students in Los Angeles, with similar ingenuity, managed to find a way around their school district's iPad security less than a week after receiving their devices and were then able to surf the Internet freely (Bloom, 2013).

From a curricular standpoint, filtering often obstructs learning and is more likely to be an unnecessary nuisance than a useful approach to keeping students away from the seamy side of the Internet, which most students, frankly, are capable of finding on their own. For learning designers, implementing a policy of teaching students how to use online access productively and encouraging on-task behaviors are more likely to yield positive results. See Chap. 14 for another aspect of this topic and two more useful resources for learning designers and policy makers, namely, a study by Grunewald Associates (2013) and a report from the American Association of School Librarians (AASL, 2012).

Capacity is the second major systemic challenge. Does the school or district have sufficient broadband capability to support the simultaneous use of, in many cases, hundreds of Internet-connected devices? Other than using their bully pulpit to advocate for necessary upgrades, learning designers may have little direct influence on capacity issues. Two current movements, however, are helping districts meet the capacity challenge. One is the implementation of the Common Core State Standards (CCSS), which has a computer-delivered testing component. Tryouts in 2013 proved less than satisfactory in some areas because of technical glitches, at least some of which were tied to capacity limitations (see Davis, 2013). While CCSS is problematic in some other ways, many school districts are actively engaged in upgrading their capacity to meet the demands of the testing component of CCSS. Such upgrades also bode well for increasing robust access to the Internet for teaching and learning.

Another positive movement is the proposed reform of E-Rate policies and procedures. The Federal Communications Commission (FCC) has engaged in discussions regarding modernization of the Schools and Libraries Program of the Universal Service Fund, known as the E-Rate, which is the subsidy program most responsible for helping schools and libraries affordably access high-capacity communication networks (see Waters, 2013). Updating and expanding the E-Rate would be a boon to districts struggling to increase their capacity to address both current and future learning needs.

Various entities have published thoughtful discussions of systemic issues, often with suggested guidelines that can be adapted for location-specific circumstances. For instance, readers may want to consult the Center for Digital Education issue brief, *Is Your K-12 Network Ready for Next-Generation Learning* (2013), or the organization's strategy paper, *Expanding Wireless in Education* (2012). The latter will be of particular interest to learning designers working in tablet classroom environments.

20.3   Device Challenges

A friend (who shall remain nameless) recently introduced me to a techie acronym: PICNIC. It stands for "problem in chair, not in computer." Most common device challenges stem from user errors: accidental touches, mistyped commands, simply trying to go faster than the device software will permit, and so forth. Tablets, given their small size and sensitive touchscreen, may be more prone to user errors than laptops or desktops, especially for less experienced users.

Simple knowledge often is the key to preventing problems. Tablet devices in particular seem to encourage unreasonable expectations of instantaneous responses across multiple, simultaneous applications. In short, expecting the tablet to do too much too fast can lead to problems, such as screen lockups and apps that suddenly close. When something doesn't work, the first response—easiest and most often effective—can be summed up in two words: try again. If an app closes unexpectedly, open it again. If the device locks up, turn it off and restart.

But what about device issues that can't be fixed so easily?

A first line of approach can be the online help site for the device in question. Every tablet manufacturer maintains a website with solutions to common problems with their devices. For example, users who experience problems with Apple's iPad can use a different computer and access the iPad Support website at http://www.apple.com/support/ipad/. There's also iPad Help at http://ipadhelp.com. And users can install an iPad Forums app (http://www.ipadforums.net) that is free from the App Store. Participants in the forums discuss problems and offer suggestions.

Google's Nexus 10 tablet users will find similar help with problems at Google's official Nexus 10 Help Center at https://support.google.com/nexus/10/?hl=en. For Android devices in general, a couple of forum sites include Android Tablets.net (http://www.androidtablets.net) and Android Central (http://www.androidcentral.com). All of these examples merely scratch the surface. An Internet search of the device name plus "help" or "support" will yield useful results.

In fact, sometimes results can be obtained simply by searching on a question. For instance, keying "Why won't my iPad turn on?" into a search engine will yield several pages of websites with possible answers to that question.

A similar approach can be used when a particular app does not work as expected. Check the app developer's website for support. If that doesn't yield results, do an Internet search on the app name plus "help" or "support," and more often than not there will be a wealth of helpful sites to consider.

These are strategies for tackling device challenges that learning designers need to know and, moreover, need to ensure that students know.

When all else fails, it's time to contact the school's instructional technology (IT) support person. If that individual cannot provide the necessary help, he or she likely can authorize contacting the manufacturer, make such contact directly, or swap the non-working device for one that works. Virtually all school districts have an IT person, who may be a school district employee or someone from a contracted service provider.

As technology becomes integral to the total operation of schools, from boardroom to classroom, many districts are mirroring business and industry by employing a chief technology officer (CTO), who is charged with overseeing technology integration overall, including ensuring effective IT support when problems arise. National Center for Education Statistics data show that about 42 % of districts with fewer than 2,500 students employ full-time CTOs. About 70 % of midsize districts do so, and the figure rises to 83 % among districts with 10,000 or more students (Cavanagh, 2013)

20.4   Usage Challenges

Learning designers can anticipate some fairly common problems when it comes to students using tablet computers because in many ways the problems are Digital Age variants on timeworn themes. Playground bullying has moved online as cyberbullying, for example. A section on safety in Chap. 14 discusses cyberbullying and so it would be redundant to include it in this section, except incidentally. Following are two other common challenges: cheating and chatting.

Cheating. The Digital Age has made it easier for today's students to cheat on classroom tests than it was for their predecessors. It's surprisingly simple for students to snap a quick photo of a test and send it to their buddies or to text a few key answers. Most tablets do not readily support the latter (texting), though there are a few apps that could be adapted to that purpose; but the camera built into many brands of tablets could facilitate the former. Learning designers might be best advised to look toward designs that encourage independent thinking and creative engagement, where there is less potential for cheating.

The idea of cheating extends to plagiarism. In the past, students copied passages for their reports verbatim from an encyclopedia; now they lift sections from Wikipedia and other websites. However, the Digital Age also has given teachers new tools for catching cheaters, such as Turnitin (http://turnitin.com), which analyzes text to identify unoriginal writing and provides teachers with an "originality report," among other services. Turnitin is available as a free iPad app.

Turnitin is one among many plagiarism checkers. Another example is Plagtracker (http://www.plagtracker.com), which is touted for students, teachers, publishers, and website owners. However, it is an online-only tool, which may make it cumbersome for tablet use except in some cases of fairly small amounts of text. It may be more useful as a teaching tool, as students can check their own writing, for example, to see whether a paraphrase is too close to the original wording of a reference passage of text.

Chatting. The teacher's lament, "I can't get the kids to stop talking so I can teach," has become "I can't get these kids to stop texting so I can teach." The ubiquity of cell phones has made texting a primary means of communication. Recall Fig. 1.1, which indicated that texting is preferred over e-mail by the under-25 age demographic. Tablets are not cell phones, of course, but they are extraordinarily like smartphones minus the phone. However, there are social networking apps that can make an actual phone function superfluous. For learning designers, the key is not to ban social networking but to turn it into an educational tool.

For example, the popularity of Facebook makes it an attractive tool for educational networking. Students can use it to share information and questions, post photos of projects, and so on. Mentoring relationships can be facilitated using the Facebook social networking platform. Researchers Pollara and Zhu (2011) found that a Facebook group that linked high school mentees and university mentors for a science project "was seen to positively affect their relationship both online and offline" (p. 3337).

A vast array of information about using Facebook in education can be found in the blogosphere, written mainly by practitioners for practitioners. A starting point for learning designers who want to incorporate social networking into teaching and learning situations is a 2009 post titled, "100 Ways You Should Be Using Facebook in Your Classroom," at http://www.onlinecollege.org/2009/10/20/100-ways-you-should-be-using-facebook-in-your-classroom/. An updated version was made 3 years later, in 2012, and can be found at http://www.onlinecollege.org/2012/05/21/100-ways-you-should-be-using-facebook-in-your-classroom-updated/. Probably needless to say, there is a Facebook page devoted to sharing information about using Facebook in education; it's at https://www.facebook.com/education.

Returning momentarily to concerns about social media and cyberbullying, Facebook took steps as of fall 2013 to provide users with a streamlined channel to report potential cyberbullying. The Facebook pilot project in Maryland was announced by that state's attorney general Doug Gansler (Associated Press, 2013b).

An alternative social networking vehicle, this one designed specifically for schools, is Edmodo (https://www.edmodo.com). This software works with a variety of computers, including iOS and Android tablets, and includes many useful, teacher-friendly features in addition to moderated social networking.

20.5   Summary

This is not a typical Q&A troubleshooting chapter because the number and variety of problems is too vast to take such an approach in any meaningful way. Rather, my hope is that learning designers understand that "trouble"—challenges and issues—are situated within the infrastructure or the device or merely in the way the device is used. The situation is key to finding appropriate solutions to the various problems.

Perhaps the best piece of advice anyone can give regarding potential challenges is to be proactive: to anticipate issues and work to avoid them. Learning designers can help schools craft sensible policies that support tablet-mediated learning and ensure that tablet classrooms are effective environments for teaching and learning. They can help schools think about capacity needs and plan accordingly.

Learning designs clearly need to incorporate time and attention to device features. In the past, effective teachers introduced their students to books: how to open them without cracking the binding, how to examine the table of contents, and how to use indexes and glossaries. Similar strategies apply to Digital Age tools, and such foreknowledge can prevent many typical device issues from arising.

Finally, the problems that arise in using tablets (or other computers) are often merely Digital Age versions of typical student management issues. It is a new age in schools, and educators are still learning—as are students—about the ins and outs of technology. Bullying, cheating, copying, and disruptive talking—all have counterparts in technology-mediated classrooms. These are not device-driven issues. They are the same old "discipline" problems schools always have faced; only the media have changed. That surreptitiously passed note is now a surreptitiously texted message.

References

AASL (American Association of School Librarians). (2012). *2012 School Libraries Count Supplemental Report on Filtering*. Chicago, IL: AASL. http://www.ala.org

Associated Press. (2013a, January 18). Ethiopian kids teach themselves with tablets. *Washington Post*. Retrieved November 13, 2013, from http://www.washingtonpost.com/lifestyle/kidspost/ethiopian-kids-teach-themselves-with-tablets/2013/01/18/7f343a3a-4a1d-11e2-b6f0-e851e741d196_story.html?tid=wp_ipad

Associated Press. (2013b, October 3). *Maryland attorney general launches pilot project with Facebook to address cyberbullying*. Washington Post. http://washingtonpost.com

Bloom, H. (2013, September 24). L.A. Students breach school iPad's security. *Los Angeles Times*. Retrieved November 13, 2013, from http://www.latimes.com/local/la-me-lausd-ipads-20130925,0,906924.story

Cavanagh, S. (2013, September 30). Many districts go without a chief tech officer. *Education Week*. Retrieved October 8, 2013, from http://www.edweek.org/ew/articles/2013/10/02/06el-cto.h33.html?tkn=VTCCBsCTQUvzbp18vh2voaZCOWRtdMguDe4D&cmp=clp-sb-ascd

Center for Digital Education. (2012). *Expanding wireless in education: Scalable network options address today's learning needs.* Folsom, CA: Author. http://www.centerdigitaled.com

Center for Digital Education. (2013). *Is your K-12 network ready for next generation learning?* Folsom, CA: Author. http://www.centerdigitaled.com

Davis, M. R. (2013, October 7). States' online testing problems raise common-core concerns. *Education Week*. Retrieved October 7, 2013, from http://www.edweek.org/ew/articles/2013/05/03/30testing.h32.html

Grunwald Associates. (2013). *Living and learning with mobile devices: What parents think about mobile devices for early childhood and K–12 learning.* San Francisco, CA: Author.

Pollara, P., & Zhu, J. (2011) Social networking and education: Using Facebook as an edusocial space. In *Proceedings of Society for Information Technology and Teacher Education International Conference 2011* (pp. 3330-3338). Chesapeake, VA: Association for the Advancement of Computing in Education. Retrieved October 9, 2011, from http://www.editlib.org/p/36833

Roscoria, T. (2011, December 19). Mobile devices prompt districts to consider security measures. Center for Digital Education. Retrieved October 7, 2013, from http://www.centerdigitaled.com/infrastructure/Mobile-Devices-Prompt-Districts-to-Consider-Security-Measures.html

Waters, J. K. (2013). The FCC must catch up with schools' needs for more and faster broadband. *THE Journal 40*, 14–19. http://thejournal.com

Index

CPSIA information can be obtained
at www.ICGtesting.com
Printed in the USA
LVOW13*0133290917

550420LV00009B/180/P